CHILDREN'S ATLAS

OF THE
BRITISH ISLES

CHILDREN'S ATLAS OF THE BRITISH ISLES

Theodore Rowland-Entwistle
and
Clare Oliver

Miles Kelly PUBLISHING

First published in 2000 by
Miles Kelly Publishing Ltd
Bardfield Centre, Great Bardfield, Essex, CM7 4SL

Copyright © 2000 Miles Kelly Publishing

2 4 6 8 10 9 7 5 3

Editor: Clare Oliver
Designer: Sally Boothroyd
Project Manager: Kate Miles
Art Director: Clare Sleven
Editorial Director: Paula Borton
Production: Rachel Jones
Artwork Commissioning: Susanne Grant, Lynne French, Natasha Smith
Picture Research: Janice Bracken, Lesley Cartlidge, Liberty Newton
Cartography: Digital Wisdom
Index: Lynn Bresler
Repro House: DPI
Additonal help from Ian Paulyn & Jane Walker

British Library Cataloguing-in-Publication Data
A catalogue record for this book is available from the British Library

ISBN 1-902947-51-7

Printed in Hong Kong

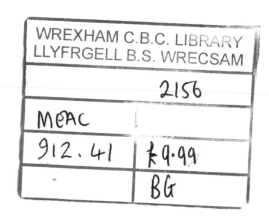
CAN YOU FIND?

Look out for these boxes as you
read this book. They suggest places
to look for on the regional maps.
Why not see if you can use the
lettered and numbered borders on
the map pages to work out map
co-ordinates for each place?
You can find out how to use map
co-ordinates on page 122.
And on page 123 you will find
answers for all the 'Can You Find?'
locations, written as co-ordinates.

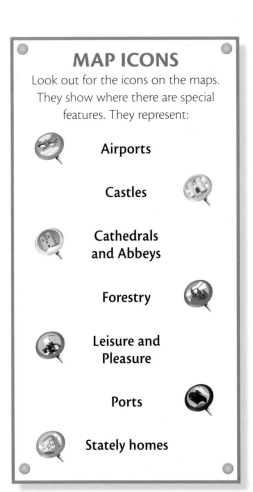

MAP ICONS

Look out for the icons on the maps.
They show where there are special
features. They represent:

Airports

Castles

Cathedrals and Abbeys

Forestry

Leisure and Pleasure

Ports

Stately homes

Contents

The British Isles

T HE BRITISH ISLES FORM THE WESTERNMOST part of Europe. They consist of two large islands, Great Britain and Ireland, the island groups of the Hebrides, Orkney, Shetland and the Scilly Isles, the Isle of Wight, the Isle of Man and Anglesey. There are also about 5,500 other small islands.

There are two nations in the British Isles. The larger one is the United Kingdom of Great Britain and Northern Ireland (UK). The other is the Republic of Ireland, which forms the southern half of Ireland. Both nations are part of the European Union (EU).

Great Britain

Great Britain consists of three historic countries: the kingdoms of England and Scotland, and the principality of Wales. The English conquered Wales in the 13th century, and the two countries were formally united in 1536. The English tried for hundreds of years to conquer Scotland. Eventually the two countries were linked when King James VI of Scotland became the heir to the English throne. Scotland retained its own parliament until 1707. In 1997 the Scots voted to have their own parliament again, and at the same time the Welsh voted to have their own national assembly. A new assembly for Northern Ireland, which had been ruled directly from Westminster since 1972, was created in 1998.

Ireland

In 1169 the Norman rulers of England laid claim to Ireland. Successive rulers tightened their grip on the country, and in 1801 Ireland was made part of the United Kingdom. At the time, the Irish were mostly Roman Catholic, but the British encouraged Protestants from Scotland and England to settle there. In 1916 a rebellion against British rule broke out in Dublin, Ireland's capital. By 1922 the southern, strongly Roman Catholic part of the island had secured independence, but the Protestants of the north voted to remain a part of the United Kingdom as the province of Northern Ireland.

▲ **Houses of Parliament, London**
This is the seat of government for the United Kingdom. It consists of the House of Commons and the House of Lords.

▲ **Leinster House, Dublin**
This is the seat of government for the Republic of Ireland. It consists of the Dáil (pronounced 'doil') and the Senate, or Seanad.

▼ **Royal residence**
The British monarch's London residence is Buckingham Palace. When the Queen is at home, the royal standard flies from the flagpole.

▼ **Days of empire**
During Victoria's reign (1837–1901), Britain's powerful overseas empire included parts of Africa, the Americas, Asia and Australasia.

▲ **Money matters**
The UK's currency is the pound sterling. Ireland's punt is being retained only until 2002: the republic has joined the EU's common currency, the euro.

▼ **James I of England**
James VI of Scotland was the son of Mary, Queen of Scots. He took the English throne in 1603 after Elizabeth I died without an heir.

WHAT'S IN A NAME?

BRITAIN
Short for 'Great Britain.'

BRITANNIA
Female warrior who symbolizes Britain; the name of the Roman province that was made up of England and Wales.

BRITISH ISLES
Geographical term referring to the European islands that lie off the north coast of France. The British Isles are made up of the two large islands of Britain and Ireland, plus thousands of smaller, often uninhabited, islands.

GREAT BRITAIN
The combined kingdoms of England and Scotland, together with the principality of Wales.

UNITED KINGDOM
Short for 'United Kingdom of Great Britain and Northern Ireland.' Political term referring to the kingdoms of England and Scotland, the principality of Wales, and Northern Ireland.

UNION JACK
The Union Jack, the United Kingdom's national flag, dates back to January 1, 1801, when the union of Ireland and Great Britain took place. The flag combines the crosses of St George of England (red on white), St Andrew of Scotland (diagonal white on blue) and St Patrick of Ireland (diagonal red on white).

NORTH
SEA

ATLANTIC
OCEAN

SCOTLAND

NORTHERN
IRELAND

IRISH
SEA

REPUBLIC
OF IRELAND

WALES

ENGLAND

0   50   100   150 Miles
0   50   100   150   200 Kilometres

ENGLISH CHANNEL

England and Wales

AS WELL AS BEING GEOGRAPHICAL NEIGHBOURS, England and Wales (Cymru in Welsh) have had close political, legal and educational links since they were united by the English king, Henry VIII, in 1536. Although Wales has been joined with England for almost 500 years, the Welsh people have kept their own language and traditions.

▲ **Roman centurion**
'Britannia' was the northernmost part of the mighty Roman Empire.

People first lived in England and Wales at least 250,000 years ago, during prehistoric times. The ancient Britons arrived before 3000BC, from what are now Spain and northern France. They were followed by the Celts from northern Europe. The Romans occupied the land for over 350 years from AD43. When they left, the Germanic Angles, Saxons and Jutes invaded. Many of the existing peoples retreated into Wales. During the 800s the Vikings conquered northern England. In 1066 William, Duke of Normandy conquered England, killing the last Saxon king, Harold II. The present queen, Elizabeth II, is descended from William.

There was Civil War in the 1600s, but the monarchy was restored in 1660. In 1707, an Act of Union joined England, Wales and Scotland to form the Kingdom of Great Britain.

▲ **Clues to history?**
Prehistoric monuments are evidence of the early Britons, but they also pose questions. For example, we do not know how, or even why, the stone circle at Stonehenge was built.

▼ St George and the Dragon by Paolo Uccello (1397–1475)

▲ **Henry VIII**
An Act of Union formally united England and Wales in 1536, during the reign of Henry VIII.

Running the country

England and Wales are part of the United Kingdom. Many of the workings of the government in London apply to the whole of the United Kingdom, but there are variations for Scotland and Northern Ireland. In 1997 the people of Wales voted for devolution, that is, the transfer of some powers of government from London to Wales. In 1999 the Welsh elected their own national assembly, to discuss Welsh affairs away from the influence of Westminster.

◄ **Patron saint of England**
George has been England's patron saint since the Middle Ages. His legendary, chivalrous deeds include slaying a dragon.

◄ Patron saint of Wales
This stained-glass window shows St David, or Dewi, who lived in the 6th century. On St David's Day, each March 1st, Welsh people honour their patron saint by wearing daffodils.

Head of State

Government is carried out in the name of the monarch, who is the head of state. The current queen is Elizabeth II, who has reigned since 1952. The king or queen has to remain outside politics. The government, with its ministers, runs the country in the Queen's name. Local government is carried out by county and unitary authorities.

Parliament

The basis of national government is Parliament. This consists of two Houses, the House of Lords and the House of Commons. The House of Lords dates to the 1300s when it was made up of powerful barons. Today it consists of peers – people who hold titles. The House of Commons holds the real power in the land. It consists of around six hundred elected members from across the United Kingdom.

Government

The head of the government is the Prime Minister. He or she is usually the leader of whichever political party holds a majority in the Commons. The Prime Minister appoints a Cabinet, a committee of about twenty senior ministers, to carry out the business of government. Cabinet ministers are in charge of departments, each responsibile for a certain sector of government. Departments include the Exchequer (finance), Foreign Office, Home Office and the Departments of Education and of Health.

WELSH LANGUAGE

In 1536 the use of the Welsh language for important matters, such as business, was banned. However, the language remained alive in the speech of ordinary people. In the 1940s Welsh became acceptable again, thanks to the efforts of the Welsh Language Society. Since 1967 Welsh can be used in court. In 1982, Wales finally got its own Welsh-language television channel, S4C. Many Welsh schools conduct lessons in both English and Welsh, and about twenty percent of the population speak the Welsh language.

◄ National emblem
Introduced by the Romans, the leek became Wales' emblem after a victorious army of Welsh-men wore the vegetable as a distinguishing 'badge' in battle.

COUNTRY FACTS

ENGLAND
Area: 130,423 sq km
Population: 49,089,100
Capital city: London
Major cities: Birmingham, Leeds, Liverpool, Manchester, Sheffield
Official language: English
Main religions: Anglicanism, Roman Catholicism, Judaism, Islam
Currency: Pound sterling (£)
Highest point: Scafell Pike (978 m)
Longest river: Thames (346 km)
Largest lake: Windermere (14.7 sq km)

WALES (CYMRU)
Area: 20,779 sq km
Population: 2,916,800
Capital city: Cardiff
Major cities and towns: Caerphilly, Newport, Swansea, Wrexham
Official languages: English, Welsh
Main religions: Anglicanism, Methodism
Currency: Pound sterling (£)
Highest point: Snowdon (1,085 m)
Longest river: Severn (partly in England) (354 km)
Largest lake: Bala (4.4 sq km)

England and Wales: Physical features

ENGLAND MAKES UP ABOUT TWO-THIRDS of the island of Great Britain, while Wales covers about ten percent of the total land area. England consists mainly of wide rolling plains, broken up by hills and moors. Wales is a chunky peninsula to the west of England. Two large islands are also part of England and Wales: Anglesey, off the North Wales coast, and the Isle of Wight, off southern England. The Scilly Isles are a group of small islands off the tip of Southwest England.

The landscape of England is more rugged in the north and in the west. The Pennine Hills run down from the Scottish border to the river Trent about halfway down the country. In the northwest is a region of mountains, hills and lakes known as the Lake District. The Midlands consist of a large plateau, bordered by the rivers Severn, Thames, Ouse and Trent. Eastern England is low and flat, with plenty of rich farmland.

The Southwest is a long peninsula with bleak moorlands and rocky outcrops. The wide expanse of Salisbury Plain occupies most of the central part of southern England. In the Southeast, a horseshoe-shaped ring of chalk downs surrounds the formerly wooded area of the Weald. The southeast corner, from Dover to Eastbourne, has dramatic chalk cliffs bordering the English Channel.

The landscape of Wales – about two-thirds of it – is covered by the Cambrian Mountains, dotted with small lakes and rivers.

▲ Hills and valleys
Much of the landscape is punctuated with rolling hills, from the gently-sloping fields and moors of Derbyshire (top) to the distinctive hummocks of Wales.

CLIMATE
The climate is mild with moderate rain, thanks to the warm-water currents of the Gulf Stream that heat the western coasts. In winter, temperatures tend to stay above 0° C and seldom fall below −10° C. The prevailing winds blow from the west across the Atlantic, bringing rain as well as warmth. They blow in a northeasterly direction and sweep up the west coast; as a result, southwest England, Wales and the Lake District have a much wetter climate than eastern England, which often suffers droughts in very hot weather. When the wind changes direction and blows from the east or from the north, it makes the weather colder, and in winter snow falls.

▼ Mount Snowdon
Snowdon, North Wales rises to 1,085 metres. Ancient glaciers carved the landscape.

▼ Fields of rape
Golden-flowered rape is a popular crop with England's farmers. The seeds are crushed to extract their oil, which is used for cooking, while the leftovers make useful animal fodder.

▲ Hills of chalk
The chalk cliffs of Sussex were formed under the sea from tiny seashells, around 142 million years ago.

NORTH SEA

IRISH SEA

ENGLISH CHANNEL

Forming the land

The rocks of England and Wales represent every period of geological time. Some time periods are named after places. The Cambrian Period gets its name from the Latin name for Wales, *Cambria*. The Devonian period, noted for its red sandstone, is named after Devon where sandstone is common. If you are interested in a spot of time travelling, the rocks of England and Wales give you the perfect opportunity! You could passing from Dorset's silvery limestone formed in the Jurassic period, through the granite masses of the Southwest, until you reached the Cambrian Mountains. There, you might even find fossils of trilobites, the earliest sea creatures with shells. The region's rocks provide different parts of England and Wales with different building materials: limestone, for example, slates from North Wales. or red bricks made from Midland clay.

▶ **Ages of the Earth**
 1 Precambrian Time: first life forms (bacteria)
 2 Cambrian Period (590 mya): oceanic shellfish, no land life
 3 Ordovician Period (505 mya): early, fish-like vertebrates
 4 Silurian Period (438 mya): first land plants
 5 Devonian Period (408 mya): first insects and amphibians
 6 Carboniferous Period (360 mya): first reptiles
 7 Permian Period (286 mya): conifers replace ferns; deserts
 8 Triassic Period (248 mya): first mammals
 9 Jurassic Period (213 mya): dinosaurs widespread
10 Cretaceous Period (144 mya): dinosaurs die out
11 Tertiary Period (65 mya): first large mammals
12 Quarternary Period (2 mya): humans evolve

London

▶ The Routemaster
London's distinctive, red double-decker buses entered service in 1959.

LONDON, THE CAPITAL CITY OF ENGLAND, is the world's ninth-largest city. Its history spans nearly 2,000 years, beginning with the arrival of the Romans soon after their invasion of Britain in AD43. London is situated on the banks of the river Thames, in Southeast England.

London consists of the ancient City of London, known simply as 'the City,' which is the business and financial heart of the United Kingdom; the City of Westminster, where Parliament and most of the government offices are located; and 31 boroughs, or local government areas, which incorporate many former towns and villages. Together they all make up a region known as Greater London, which has an area of 1,580 square kilometres and a population of 6,767,500.

▲ London at night
The domes of St Paul's are lit up at night. The cathedral was built by Christopher Wren after the Great Fire of 1666.

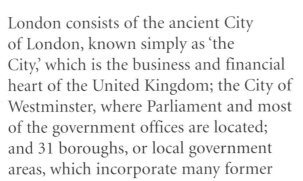

▲ Lloyd's Building
Designed by Richard Rogers in 1986, the Lloyd's Building dominates the City of London's skyline.

London is a major port, although its importance has diminished since the end of World War II. It has three airports which are all located outside the city area: Heathrow, Gatwick and Stansted. London is the hub of the United Kingdom's rail network, with about a dozen mainline railway terminuses.

▲ London Boroughs
London is so large it is divided into separate administrative areas called boroughs.

Important buildings

London is packed with buildings and other sites of historical interest. The most important buildings include the Tower of London, which was begun in 1078 by William the Conqueror. It is London's only surviving castle. Buckingham Palace is the official home of the monarch, while the nearby Palace of St James is the official address of the royal court. Other royal palaces include Kensington Palace and Hampton Court. The Palace of Westminster is the official name of the Houses of Parliament. Lambeth Palace is the home of the Archbishop of Canterbury.

St Paul's Cathedral, with its famous domed towers, is one of London's most famous churches. It is in the heart of the City of London. London's other well-known church is Westminster Abbey.

Edward the Confessor began work on its construction over 900 years ago. England's kings and queens have been crowned in Westminster Abbey for hundreds of years, and many other state ceremonies are held there.

Moments in history

The Romans founded London in about AD43. It has grown rapidly since the arrival of William the Conqueror in 1066. A disastrous fire in 1666 destroyed the original St Paul's Cathedral, 89 parish churches and 13,000 houses in the City of London. During World War II, the Blitz (enemy air raids) of London in 1940–1 destroyed huge areas of the city, especially around the docks. As the bombed areas were gradually rebuilt, London began to spread upwards as well as outwards. Huge skyscrapers appeared and tall blocks of flats began to reshape the whole skyline of the city.

▲ **Tower Bridge**
The Thames snakes through the capital. Several bridges link north and south London.

◄ **Royal Albert Hall**
This concert hall was built by Queen Victoria to commemorate her husband, Prince Albert. Each summer it hosts a highly-popular musical festival, the Proms.

◄ **Regent's Park Zoo**
London Zoo, opened in 1828, houses rare species and does vital conservation work. The walk-through aviary features many exotic birds and was designed by Lord Snowdon.

▶ **10 Downing Street**
A policeman, or 'bobby,' stands guard at No. 10 Downing Street. This is the London residence of the British Prime Minister.

The Southwest

▼ Exmoor

NUMEROUS VISITORS COME to the Southwest of England, attracted by the region's natural beauty and mild climate. Its scenery ranges from the wide-open spaces of Devon to Cornwall's pretty fishing villages, and from the rolling hills of Dorset to the beautiful stone cottages that nestle in the Cotswolds.

Cornwall, Devon and Somerset form a peninsula, bounded to the north by the Bristol Channel, and to the south by the English Channel. The wild granite plateau of Dartmoor in Devon, with its rocky outcrops, dramatic gorges and valleys, is a national park. Further north, another national park, the bracken-covered hilly moorland of Exmoor, reaches across Somerset and North Devon. To the east, Salisbury Plain in Wiltshire is a vast grassland with areas set aside for military use. The region's main rivers are the Severn, Britain's longest river, which empties into the Bristol Channel, and the Avon, which flows through the city of Bristol.

Important towns

Bristol is the region's biggest city, and is also an important port whose fortunes were founded in the 1700s on the slave trade. Slaves were brought here from West Africa. Smaller ports in the region include Weymouth, Poole and Plymouth, from where Sir Francis Drake set sail in 1588 to fight the Spanish Armada. Ferry services to continental Europe operate from all these ports. Other important cities and towns include the Roman cities of Bath and Gloucester, and the historic cathedral cities of Exeter and Salisbury. The Southwest has six universities: at Bath, Bournemouth, Bristol (two), Exeter and Plymouth.

▲ **Sand martin**
Cotswold Water Park is Britain's biggest artificial wetland. Sand martins visit the Cotswolds in early summer each year.

BRILLIANT BRIDGE

Bristol's Clifton Suspension Bridge, designed by the Victorian engineering genius Isambard Kingdom Brunel, has spanned the Avon Gorge since 1864. It is a dizzying 75 metres high.

▼ **Dino remains**
Lyme Regis is the fossil-collecting capital of the British Isles. Its shingle beach and limestone cliffs are rich in the fossilised remains of dinosaurs and other prehistoric creatures.

◀ **Ammonite fossil**

Lundy Island

Hartland Point

ATLANTIC OCEAN

Hartland

Bude Bay • Bude

Tamar

Tintagel Castle
• Tintagel

Port Isaac

Launcesto

Trevose Head

BODMIN MOOR

Padstow

Allen

Bodmin

Camel

Fowey

Liske

Newquay • St Columb Major

Looe

Fal

St. Austell

St Agnes Head • St Agnes

Truro

Mevagissy

Dodman Point

• St Ives • Redruth

St Just

St Michael's Mount

Falmouth • • St Mawes

Land's End

Penzance

• Helston

Sennen

Manacle Point

Isles of Scilly

• Lizard

Lizard Point

COUNTY FACTS

CORNWALL
Area: 3,545 sq km
Population: 482,700
Administrative centre: Truro
Other key places: Newquay, St Ives

DEVON
Area: 6,710 sq km
Population: 378,900
Administrative centre: Exeter
Other key places: Plymouth, Torbay

DORSET
Area: 2,655 sq km
Population: 378,900
Administrative centre: Dorchester
Other key places: Bournemouth, Poole

GLOUCESTERSHIRE
Area: 2,643 sq km
Population: 552,700
Administrative centre: Gloucester
Other key places: Bristol, Cheltenham

SOMERSET
Area: 3,450 sq km
Population: 481,000
Administrative centre: Taunton
Other key places: Bridgwater, Burnham, Cheddar, Minehead

WILTSHIRE
Area: 3,480 sq km
Population: 416,000
Administrative centre: Trowbridge
Other key places: Marlborough, Swindon, Warminster

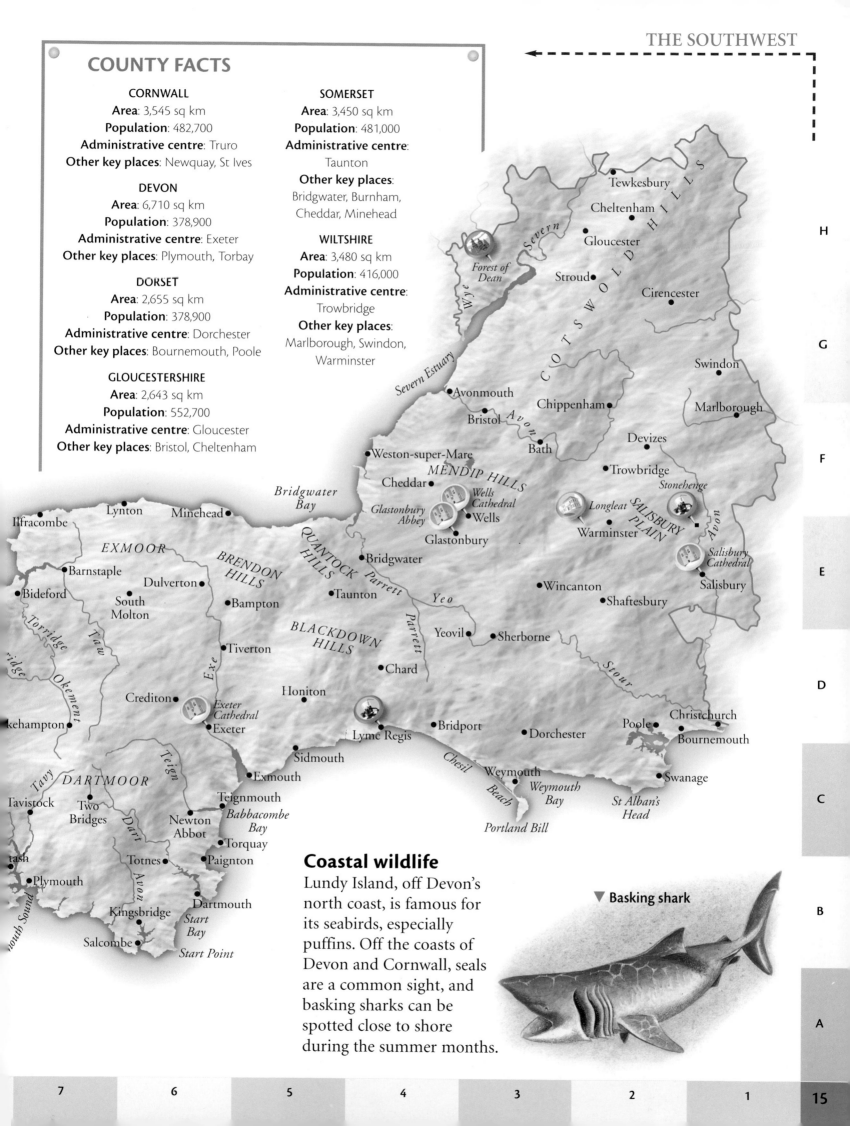

Tewkesbury
Cheltenham
Gloucester
Stroud
Cirencester
COTSWOLD HILLS
Swindon
Marlborough
Chippenham
Bristol
Avon
Bath
Devizes
Avonmouth
Severn Estuary
Wye
Forest of Dean
Severn
Weston-super-Mare
Trowbridge
Stonehenge
MENDIP HILLS
Cheddar
Wells Cathedral
Wells
Longleat
SALISBURY PLAIN
Glastonbury Abbey
Glastonbury
Warminster
Salisbury Cathedral
Salisbury
Bridgwater Bay
QUANTOCK HILLS
Bridgwater
Parrett
Yeo
Wincanton
Shaftesbury
Lynton
Minehead
Taunton
EXMOOR
BRENDON HILLS
Parrett
Yeovil
Sherborne
Stour
Ilfracombe
Barnstaple
Dulverton
Bampton
BLACKDOWN HILLS
Chard
Bideford
South Molton
Torridge
Taw
Exe
Tiverton
Honiton
Bridport
Dorchester
Poole
Christchurch
Bournemouth
Crediton
Exeter Cathedral
Exeter
Lyme Regis
Sidmouth
Weymouth
Swanage
Okement
kehampton
Teign
Exmouth
Chesil Beach
Weymouth Bay
St Alban's Head
Tavy
DARTMOOR
Teignmouth
Babbacombe Bay
Portland Bill
Tavistock
Two Bridges
Newton Abbot
Torquay
Dart
Totnes
Paignton
tash
Avon
Plymouth
Dartmouth
Start Bay
Kingsbridge
Salcombe
Start Point
mouth Sound

Coastal wildlife

Lundy Island, off Devon's north coast, is famous for its seabirds, especially puffins. Off the coasts of Devon and Cornwall, seals are a common sight, and basking sharks can be spotted close to shore during the summer months.

▼ **Basking shark**

H
G
F
E
D
C
B
A

7   6   5   4   3   2   1   **15**

REMAINS OF STONE AGE PEOPLE have been found in several places in Gloucestershire. Somerset's oldest inhabitants included Iron Age people whose remains have been discovered in limestone caves at Wookey Hole, near Cheddar.

▲ Circle of stones
Stonehenge was erected at about the same time as the Great Pyramids at Giza in Egypt. No one is sure of the monument's purpose, but it was probably connected with worship of the Sun.

The Southwest has one of the world's finest ancient monuments, Stonehenge on Salisbury Plain in Wiltshire. Other Stone Age sites include nearby Avebury Rings and Silbury Hill, a huge artificial hill built of turf.

▼ The Roman Baths
There are three natural hot springs at Bath, supplying the Great Bath, the King's Bath and the Roman Baths.

▲ Tintagel Castle, Cornwall

HISTORIC BUILDINGS

BERKELEY CASTLE, GLOUCESTERSHIRE
At this medieval castle, Edward II was killed with a red-hot poker in 1327.

EXETER CATHEDRAL, DEVON
The north tower of this ornate cathedral houses an astronomical clock that shows the phases of the Moon.

LACOCK ABBEY, WILTSHIRE
In 1835 Henry Fox Talbot took the first negative photograph here.

LONGLEAT HOUSE, WILTSHIRE
Longleat's attractions include a safari park and a library of 40,000 books.

TINTAGEL CASTLE, CORNWALL
Magical ruins are all that remain of King Arthur's castle.

WELLS CATHEDRAL, SOMERSET
This Gothic cathedral's west front features over 300 carved figures.

▶ King Arthur

Amazing legends
The Southwest has many connections with the legendary King Arthur. Tintagel Castle in Cornwall is believed to be Arthur's birthplace, and the ancient hill fort of Cadbury was long thought to be one of his residences. Glastonbury is said to be the king's burial place. According to legend, Glastonbury Abbey, now in ruins, was founded by Joseph of Arimathea, a follower of Jesus Christ. Joseph is said to have brought the Holy Grail (the cup used at the Last Supper) to England.

Spa town
The city of Bath stands over naturally hot springs and the Romans visited the city as a health resort. Many of the public baths they built there are still intact, and it is from these that the town gets its name. Other Roman cities in the region are Gloucester and Cheltenham.

▼ Going supersonic

Concorde, which made its maiden flight in 1969, was the first passenger plane to break the sound barrier. It was assembled and tested in Bristol.

All at sea

Bristol has strong seafaring links. Italian-born explorer John Cabot set sail from Bristol in 1497 in his ship, *The Matthew*. He reached the coast of Newfoundland, and was the first European since the Vikings to set foot on North American soil. Almost 400 years later, another famous ship, the SS *Great Britain*, steamed out of Bristol. Designed by the engineer Isambard Kingdom Brunel, this screw-propelled passenger ship was the largest in the world when launched in 1843. Today, it lies preserved at Bristol.

◄ John Cabot

On reaching Newfoundland, Cabot unfurled two flags: a British flag that claimed the land for Henry VII, and the flag of his home-town, Venice, in Italy.

CAN YOU FIND?

1 Bristol
2 Longleat House
3 Lyme Regis
4 St Ives

see pages 14 and 15

▲ Wookey Hole

The Mendip Hills have many underground caves, most famously at Wookey Hole and at Cheddar Cliffs. The rock of the region is limestone, which is worn away and hollowed out by underground streams.

► Abstract art

The beautiful seaside town of St Ives is home to many artists. Sculptress Dame Barbara Hepworth lived there until her death in 1975. Today, her house is a museum of her works.

Industry

Cornwall used to be famous for its tin mines, which operated from Roman times until the last mine closed in 1998. There are stone and clay quarries in Devon and Cornwall. Other regional industries include engineering, shipbuilding, electronics and food processing. Swindon is home to many new industries, such as computers. Japanese car manufacturer Honda has an important car plant just outside the town.

◄ St Michael's Mount

A castle tops St Michael's Mount, a small rocky island off Cornwall's south coast. It is situated between Lizard Point, England's most southerly point, and Land's End, the most westerly point.

▲ Animation success

The award-winning cartoon duo Wallace and Gromit were created by animator Nick Park using a process called claymation at the Aardman studios in Bristol.

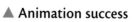

The Southeast

▼ **Badger setts**
The New Forest, Hampshire, is a good place to observe badgers. There is floodlighting and a cut-away glass-fronted sett on view.

THE SOUTHEAST OF ENGLAND is one of the most crowded parts of the country. In the centre of the region lies the bustling city of London, capital of the whole of the United Kingdom. Many people who live in the Southeast are commuters – they travel to work in the capital each day but live in the surrounding counties.

The Southeast is surrounded by water on three sides: to the south is the English Channel, to the east and southeast lies the Strait of Dover, and to the north flows the river Thames to its estuary. The North and South Downs are an important feature of the local landscape. This horseshoe-shaped range of hills stretches across the counties of Kent, Surrey and Sussex, and reaches partly into Hampshire. Two famous landmarks are formed where the Downs meet the coastline: the world-famous White Cliffs at Dover, and the towering chalk cliffs of Seven Sisters, in East Sussex. The lowland area inside the 'horseshoe' of the Downs is known as the Weald and was once covered in woods.

▲ **Seven Sisters**
As the chalk cliffs of the south coast erode, they form breathtaking shapes, such as the Seven Sisters in East Sussex.

▼ **Ramblers on the Downs**

Important towns

The M25, the motorway which rings London, is linked by other motorways with the Channel ports of Dover, Southampton and Portsmouth. Dover is England's busiest port. Ferries carry passengers and freight to and from the continent of Europe. The ports of Newhaven and Ramsgate also operate ferry services, and there is an important naval base at Portsmouth. The terminus for the Channel Tunnel, which opened in 1994 and links the English mainland with the rest of Europe, is at Folkestone. There are several busy seaside resorts in the Southeast, including Worthing, Brighton, Eastbourne, Hastings and Margate. The cathedral towns of Winchester and Canterbury also attract many visitors each year.

◄ **The *Titanic***
This 'unsinkable' liner sailed from Southampton in 1912. About 1,500 people lost their lives after an iceberg pierced the ship's hull, and it sank.

Andover
Winchester Cathedral
Test
Winchester
Avon
New Forest
Southampto
Lymington
The Solent
Newpo
Isle
Wi
St Catherine's Po

COUNTY FACTS

HAMPSHIRE
Area: 3,780 sq km
Population: 1,213,400
Administrative centre: Winchester
Other key places: Basingstoke, Gosport, Portsmouth, Southampton

ISLE OF WIGHT
Area : 380 sq km
Population : 125,100
Administrative centre: Newport
Other key places: Cowes, Ryde, Sandown, Shanklin

KENT
Area : 3,760 sq km
Population : 1,551,300
Administrative centre: Maidstone
Other key places: Canterbury, Dover, Margate, Royal Tunbridge Wells

SURREY
Area : 1,665 sq km
Population : 1,004,000
Administrative centre: Kingston-upon-Thames (now in Greater London)
Other key places: Guildford, Reigate

EAST SUSSEX
Area : 1,796 sq km
Population : 1,577,000
Administrative centre: Lewes
Other key places: Brighton, Eastbourne, Hastings, Newhaven, Uckfield

WEST SUSSEX
Area : 2,015 sq km
Population : 731,500
Administrative centre: Chichester
Other key places: Bognor Regis, Crawley, East Grinstead, Worthing

The Channel Tunnel

Boring a rail tunnel to link the British Isles to mainland Europe began in 1987. In 1994 Eurotunnel opened. There are really three tunnels, not one. Two are for rail traffic and the other is for services and security. Trains travel through the tunnel at speeds of 160 kilometres per hour and the trip under the Channel takes about 35 minutes.

◄ Brighton rock

► Bee orchid

RARE FLOWERS

The chalky Downs provide the perfect conditions for wild orchids. These include the lady orchid and the bee orchid, so-called because it attracts bees on the lookout for a mate.

THE EARLIEST KNOWN INHABITANT of the Southeast was 'Swanscombe Man,' whose skull was found at Swanscombe, Kent. He is thought to be at least 100,000 years old. Another skull was found at Piltdown, in East Sussex, in the 1920s. This find caused much excitement but it later turned out to be a fake.

▲ Julius Caesar

Ancient trackways and hill forts show us that ancient Britons lived in this region thousands of years ago. The Roman general Julius Caesar invaded the area twice, in 55BC and again the following year. But he returned to Gaul (modern France) without achieving much. The main Roman invasion took place in AD43, when Emperor Claudius sent three armies – and large numbers of elephants – to occupy England. The remains of huge Roman villas (country houses) have been found at Lullingstone, Kent and at Fishbourne near Chichester, West Sussex.

ST SWITHIN'S DAY

St Swithin's Day is on July 15th each year. The saying goes that if it rains on this day, it will rain for another 40. The day is named after St Swithin, the Bishop of Winchester, Hampshire. On July 15, AD971 his body was dug up to be moved to another cathedral, but heavy rains delayed the move.

THE CINQUE PORTS

The original Cinque (from the French word *cinq*, meaning 'five') Ports were Dover, Hastings, Hythe, Romney and Sandwich. From 1278 they supplied the monarch with ships in return for special privileges. They were later joined by Rye and Winchelsea.

The Anglo Saxons

After the Romans left, the Angles and Saxons from Germany invaded. The first to arrive in southeast England were the legendary warriors Hengest and Horsa, who landed at Ebbsfleet, Kent. The Anglo Saxons quickly spread over the region. Their rule came to an end in 1066 when William of Normandy defeated the Saxon king, Harold II, at Battle, near Hastings.

▼ To be a pilgrim
The 13th-century poet Geoffrey Chaucer is best-known for his *Canterbury Tales*. It is written as a collection of stories told by pilgrims on their way to Canterbury.

Cathedral city

Canterbury Cathedral, which has a magnificent central tower, is known as the Mother Church of England. Its archbishop is the head of the English church. Pilgrims have visited the city since medieval times, when Thomas Becket was murdered inside the cathedral by the English king, Henry II.

▲ **1066 and all that**
English history changed forever when William, Duke of Normandy, defeated King Harold in 1066 at Battle, E.Sussex.

CASTLES

DOVER CASTLE, KENT
Within the stone walls of this fortress are the ruins of Britain's oldest building, a Roman lighthouse called the Pharos.

HEVER CASTLE, KENT
In the grounds of this moated Tudor castle, family home of Anne Boleyn, are a yew-hedge maze and a water maze.

LEEDS CASTLE, KENT
Henry VIII turned the original 9th-century fortress, standing on two islets in a lake, into a fairytale palace.

PEVENSEY CASTLE, EAST SUSSEX
This Norman castle was built within the walls of a Roman fort, called Anderida, which dates back to AD250.

SISSINGHURST CASTLE, KENT
This Elizabethan mansion with a moat was home to the writer and gardener Vita Sackville-West. You can still visit her famous 'White Garden.'

Famous buildings

There are a number of stately homes in the Southeast, such as Knole in Sevenoaks. Chartwell Manor, which was the country estate of Sir Winston Churchill, houses lots of Churchill memorabilia. One of the region's most remarkable buildings is the Royal Pavilion at Brighton, which was built as a seaside palace for the Prince Regent, later King George IV. With its onion-shaped dome and Chinese interior, the Pavilion is an amazing mixture of oriental and Moorish styles.

Industry and farming

The Southeast has many light industries and is also home to Britain's largest oil refinery at Fawley, near Southampton. There are hovercraft factories on the Isle of Wight. Kent has paper mills, shipyards, and a nuclear power station at Dungeness. Away from the towns, there are hundreds of small farms, with orchards and fruit farms. Kent, known as the 'Garden of England,' is famous for its apples and for hops, used in brewing beer. Lamberhurst is known for its vineyards and produces English wines.

◄ **19th-century novelist**
Charles Dickens, who wrote *A Christmas Carol*, was born in Kent. There are Dickens museums at Canterbury and Broadstairs.

▶ **Hop houses**
Oast houses dot the countryside of Kent and East Sussex. Once, hops were dried in these giant kilns. Today, many are private homes.

▼ **The Royal Pavilion, Brighton**

CAN YOU FIND?

1 Canterbury Cathedral
2 Cowes
3 Leeds Castle
4 New Forest
5 Thorpe Park

see pages 18 and 19

South Central

Epping Forest, Essex, covers 345 square kilometres. The rich clay soil supports hardwood trees, such as beech, oak and ash.

▼ Berkshire Downs

THIS REGION IS SOMETIMES CONSIDERED part of southeast England. Its counties lie to the north and east of London and many of the people living here commute to London to work.

South Central England is a mix of lowlands and chains of small hills. To the west are the Cotswold Hills, while the Chilterns extend from Oxfordshire across Buckinghamshire into Hertfordshire. The Vale of the White Horse lies in southern Oxfordshire and northern Berkshire. It is bordered to the south by the White Horse Hills and the Berkshire Downs. The river Thames and its tributary, the Cherwell, flow east towards London, passing through the beautiful, tree-lined Goring Gap between the Berkshire Downs and the Chilterns. The rest of the region is low-lying, especially Essex. This county has marshy land along its ragged North Sea coast and along the Thames estuary. The rivers Blackwater, Colne and Crouch flow east toward the sea, while other rivers in the region are tributaries of the Thames.

▼ Education for all

Milton Keynes is the headquarters of the Open University, whose students get their degrees by correspondence courses.

Important towns

Oxford is the largest city in the region and is home to one of Britain's oldest universities. Other important towns include Reading and Windsor in Berkshire, St Albans and Watford in Hertfordshire, and Colchester (one of England's oldest towns) and Chelmsford in Essex.

The London orbital motorway, the M25, runs through South Central England, with other motorways radiating from it. The M25 links with its southern half at the Dartford Crossing, where there are a mixture of tunnels and a suspension bridge. Stansted, one of London's three airports, is in Essex.

▲ Web-footed wader

Abberton Reservoir in Essex is home to many water birds, including cormorants (*above*) and common terns.

Banbury

Chipping
• Norton

Blenheim Palace

Thames Oxfo
Abingdon •

VALE OF THE
WHITE HORSE

BERKSHI
Newbury •

◀ Days on the river

Oxford sits on the river Cherwell. For a fine view of the countryside that surrounds the city, hire a flat-bottomed boat, called a punt.

Stansted Airport

Top British architect Norman Foster designed London's newest airport at Stansted, which opened in 1993. The low, single-storey building has glass walls that allow travellers to see the sky, the runways and the fields beyond.

FLOWER POWER

The town of Saffron Walden in Essex takes its name from the fields of saffron crocuses that were grown there from medieval times. It takes 165,000 flowers to produce just one kilogram of saffron.

COUNTY FACTS

BERKSHIRE
Area: 1,260 sq km
Population: 783,200
Administrative centre: Reading
Other key places: Maidenhead, Newbury, Slough, Windsor

BUCKINGHAMSHIRE
Area: 1,883 sq km
Population: 473,000
Administrative centre: Aylesbury
Other key places: High Wycombe, Milton Keynes

ESSEX
Area: 3,685 sq km
Population: 1,557,500
Administrative centre: Chelmsford
Other key places: Basildon, Colchester, Harwich

HERTFORDSHIRE
Area: 1,636 sq km
Population: 1,001,200
Administrative centre: Hertford
Other key places: Hemel Hempstead, St Albans, Stevenage

OXFORDSHIRE
Area: 2,620 sq km
Population: 598,400
Administrative centre: Oxford
Other key places: Abingdon, Banbury, Eynsham

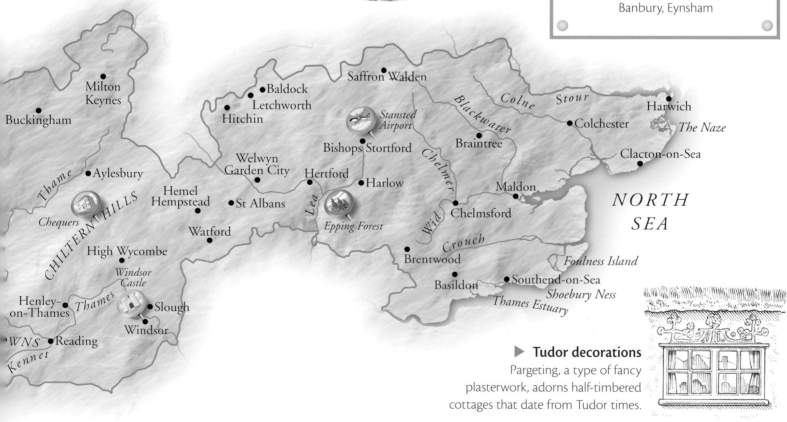

▶ **Tudor decorations**
Pargeting, a type of fancy plasterwork, adorns half-timbered cottages that date from Tudor times.

▲ The White Horse

PREHISTORIC PEOPLE HAVE LEFT THEIR MARK on this region. There are several stone circles in Oxfordshire, including one known as the Rollright Stones which consists of around 70 well-worn stones.

CAN YOU FIND?
1 Banbury   4 St Albans
2 Colchester   5 Windsor
3 Milton Keynes
                 see page 23

Above the Vale of the White Horse in the Berkshire Downs, cut into the turf of the chalk hills, is the dramatic carved horse that gives the area its name. Recent research has proved that it was made 3,000 years ago during the Bronze Age. About 2,000 years older than the White Horse is the Icknield Way, a prehistoric hill track that follows the line of the chalk hills through Berkshire.

In Roman times

The Romans built important roads through the region, and there are the remains of several villas. They also developed two key towns, Verulamium (St Albans) and Camulodunum (Colchester). You can still see the Roman theatre and parts of the ancient city walls on the outskirts of St Albans. In Essex the Romans fought against ancient British tribes, notably the Trinovantes. The Saxon kingdoms of Wessex and Mercia occupied the region at various times, and the Vikings invaded and occupied during the AD800s.

Castles

The royal residence of Windsor Castle is the region's most impressive castle, and the only one intact. Its 24-metre-high round keep is visible from the London Eye ferris wheel. The bodies of several English kings, including Henry VIII and George VI, lie buried in Windsor Castle's chapel.

▲ Boudicca
In AD60 the warrior queen of the Iceni tribe sacked the Roman settlement at Colchester, Essex.

▲ Henry VIII

◀ Up in flames
A fire broke out in the royal library at Windsor in November 1992. All the art treasures were saved but the castle needed costly restoration work because of the fire – and the water used to extinguish it.

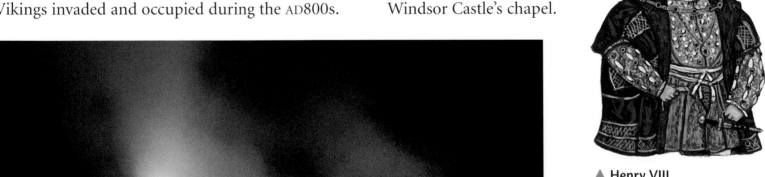

Famous buildings and landmarks

The most magnificent of the region's stately homes is Blenheim Palace, Oxfordshire. It was built for the victorious General John Churchill, first Duke of Marlborough. Chequers, in Buckinghamshire, is a Tudor mansion that is used as a country retreat by the British prime minister. Audley End House, a Jacobean mansion in Essex, was used as a royal palace by Charles II. Essex also boasts Europe's oldest timber building, St Andrew's Church, Greensted. Its nave is made from oak trunks that date back to AD850.

▲ Charles II

▼ Brickloads of fun
Legoland Windsor is home to model masterpieces made entirely from plastic Lego building bricks.

▲ Jingle bells!
Since medieval times, Morris dancers have entertained us on special occasions, such as May Day. They wear colourful costumes and often tie bells to their legs!

Industry and farming

Industry in Berkshire centres around Bracknell (home of the Meteorological Office), Maidenhead, Reading and Slough, with electronics concentrated in Milton Keynes. Hertfordshire is known for engineering, mostly at St Albans, Hatfield, Letchworth and Watford. The Oxford suburb of Cowley has huge car factories and was the birthplace of the classic Morris Minor. Essex has shipbuilding at Tilbury, and an oil refinery near Canvey Island, but much of the county is farmland, with lots of fruit orchards.

▲ Morris Minor

WHAT'S IN A NAME?
William Spooner, warden of New College, Oxford, was famous for muddling his words. He once told off a student, saying "You have deliberately tasted two worms and can leave Oxford by the town drain". To this day, sentences in which the first letters of the words have been mixed up are called Spoonerisms.

West Midlands

▼ Deepest Derbyshire
Farmers' fields give way to the moorlands of the Peak District.

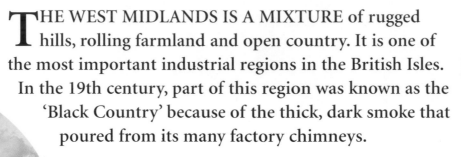

THE WEST MIDLANDS IS A MIXTURE of rugged hills, rolling farmland and open country. It is one of the most important industrial regions in the British Isles. In the 19th century, part of this region was known as the 'Black Country' because of the thick, dark smoke that poured from its many factory chimneys.

▲ The bard
The most famous English playwright, William Shakespeare, was born at Stratford-upon-Avon in 1564. His plays included *Romeo and Juliet* and *Hamlet.*

The region has some spectacular scenery. To the west, the valleys of the rivers Wye and Severn cross the Malvern Hills. Further east, in north Staffordshire, lie the foothills of the Pennines. In these rugged hills lies the Peak District National Park, with its peaty bogs and moors and beautiful dales. To the south is Cannock Chase, a mixture of moors and woods. The large expanse of Rutland Water is a feature of the eastern side of this region. In the south are the high plateau of the West Midlands and the rolling hills of Warwickshire, separated from the Cotswolds by the river Avon.

▼ Spaghetti Junction
Seen from above, it is not hard to see how this complex intersection of roads and motorways outside Birmingham got its nickname!

Important towns

In the heart of the West Midlands lies the city of Birmingham, a major centre of industry and the arts. Stratford-upon-Avon, Warwickshire, is famous as the birthplace of the writer William Shakespeare. Hereford, Derby, Warwick and Worcester are historic cities with many fine buildings. There is a total of 13 universities in the West Midlands: at Birmingham (three), Coventry (two), Derby, Leicester (two), Loughborough, Newcastle-under-Lyme, Stafford, Stoke-on-Trent and Wolverhampton.

▲ Bluebell woods
One of the best places to see the springtime display of English bluebells is at Saltwells Wood, near Dudley, West Midlands.

▶ Across the river
This viaduct at Monsal Dale, Derbyshire, was built by the Romans.

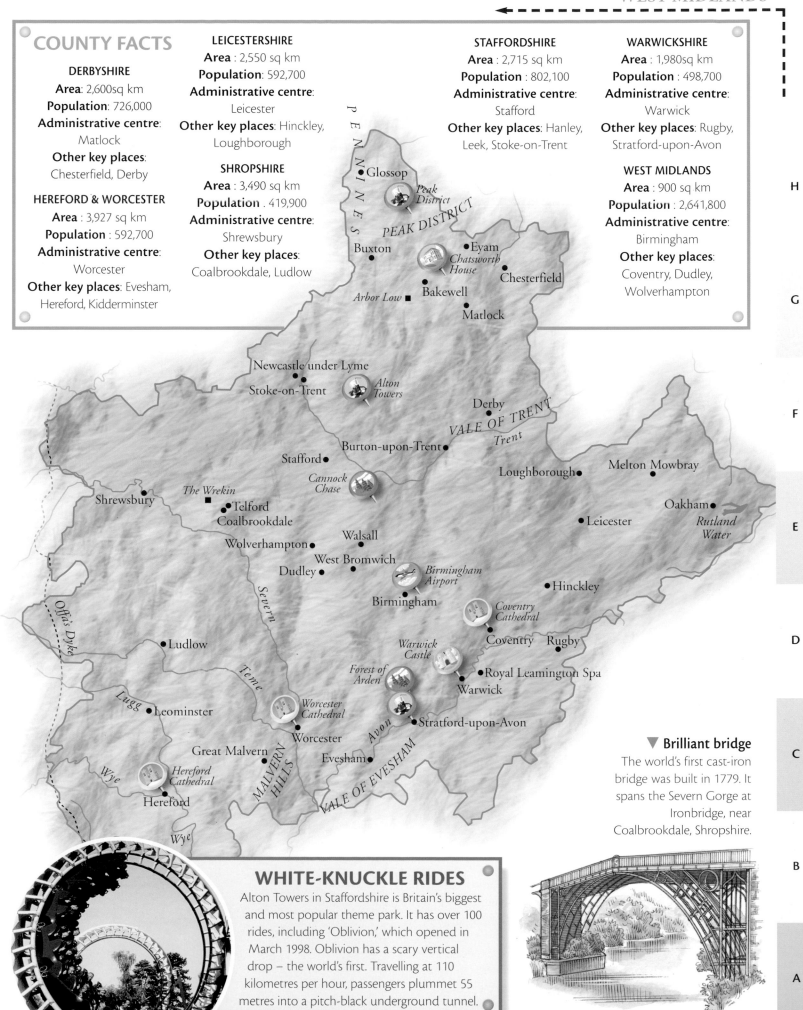

COUNTY FACTS

DERBYSHIRE
Area: 2,600sq km
Population: 726,000
Administrative centre: Matlock
Other key places: Chesterfield, Derby

HEREFORD & WORCESTER
Area : 3,927 sq km
Population : 592,700
Administrative centre: Worcester
Other key places: Evesham, Hereford, Kidderminster

LEICESTERSHIRE
Area : 2,550 sq km
Population: 592,700
Administrative centre: Leicester
Other key places: Hinckley, Loughborough

SHROPSHIRE
Area : 3,490 sq km
Population . 419,900
Administrative centre: Shrewsbury
Other key places: Coalbrookdale, Ludlow

STAFFORDSHIRE
Area : 2,715 sq km
Population : 802,100
Administrative centre: Stafford
Other key places: Hanley, Leek, Stoke-on-Trent

WARWICKSHIRE
Area : 1,980sq km
Population : 498,700
Administrative centre: Warwick
Other key places: Rugby, Stratford-upon-Avon

WEST MIDLANDS
Area : 900 sq km
Population : 2,641,800
Administrative centre: Birmingham
Other key places: Coventry, Dudley, Wolverhampton

PENNINES

Glossop

Peak District

PEAK DISTRICT

Buxton

Eyam

Chatsworth House

Chesterfield

Arbor Low ■ Bakewell

Matlock

Newcastle under Lyme

Stoke-on-Trent

Alton Towers

Derby

VALE OF TRENT

Trent

Burton-upon-Trent

Stafford

Cannock Chase

Loughborough

Melton Mowbray

Shrewsbury

The Wrekin ■

Telford
Coalbrookdale

Oakham

Rutland Water

Leicester

Wolverhampton

Walsall

West Bromwich

Dudley

Severn

Birmingham Airport

Hinckley

Birmingham

Offa's Dyke

Ludlow

Teme

Coventry Cathedral

Warwick Castle

Coventry

Rugby

Lugg

Leominster

Forest of Arden

Royal Leamington Spa

Warwick

Worcester Cathedral

Great Malvern

Wye

Hereford Cathedral

Hereford

Worcester

MALVERN HILLS

Avon

Stratford-upon-Avon

Evesham

VALE OF EVESHAM

Wye

WHITE-KNUCKLE RIDES
Alton Towers in Staffordshire is Britain's biggest and most popular theme park. It has over 100 rides, including 'Oblivion,' which opened in March 1998. Oblivion has a scary vertical drop – the world's first. Travelling at 110 kilometres per hour, passengers plummet 55 metres into a pitch-black underground tunnel.

▼ Brilliant bridge
The world's first cast-iron bridge was built in 1779. It spans the Severn Gorge at Ironbridge, near Coalbrookdale, Shropshire.

H

G

F

E

D

C

B

A

THE WEST MIDLANDS HAS MANY ANCIENT SITES. Arbor Low, a stone circle on a windy hilltop in Derbyshire, was built about 2000BC. It is surrounded by many graves from the Bronze Age. Stone Age hunters once lived in the caves of Creswell Crags, a narrow gorge near Worksop.

▲ **Cave life**
Prehistoric people found ready-made homes in the caves at Creswell Crags.

▲ **Offa's Dyke**
This 270-kilometre-long embankment was 18 metres high in places.

▼ **It's a knockout!**
One of the favourite entertainments at a medieval castle was the jousting tournament. In a make-believe battle, two armed knights charged at each other. The first to 'unhorse' the other with his lance was the winner!

The Romans lived in this area and built several roads through it, which are still in use today. The Anglo Saxons established the powerful kingdom of Mercia in the AD500s. Offa's Dyke, a ditch and rampart that marked the border between England and Wales, was built by King Offa of Mercia in the 700s. In the 800s, Vikings occupied the area. They were generally known as the Danes, and the West Midlands became part of their territory called the Danelaw. It came under Norman control after 1066.

CAN YOU FIND?
1 Eyam
2 Loughborough
3 Rugby
4 Stratford-upon-Avon
5 Worcester

see page 27

Famous castles

In medieval times, Edward I and his barons built a chain of castles along the border with Wales in an effort to keep Welsh rebels under control. Running from north to south, the castles include Shrewsbury, Whittington, Moreton Corbet and Acton Burnell. There are several castles from earlier times, too. Warwick Castle was converted from a grim Norman fortress to a stately home in the 1600s. Kenilworth Castle, in Warwickshire, is famous for the mysterious death of Amy, wife to Elizabeth I's favourite, the Earl of Leicester. Amy was said to have committed suicide, but many people suspected that Leicester himself was involved in her death.

VILLAGE OF DEATH
Eyam, Derbyshire, is known as the 'Plague Village.' The bubonic plague broke out there in 1665, after being carried from London in a box of cloth sent to Eyam's tailor. The 350 villagers bravely isolated themselves so that the disease would not spread. By the time the epidemic ended, 262 of them had lost their lives.

▶ **Into the scrum**
In the 19th century Rugby School, Warwickshire, gave its name to a brand-new ball-game. During a football match, one school-boy picked up the ball and ran with it, and the sport of rugby was born.

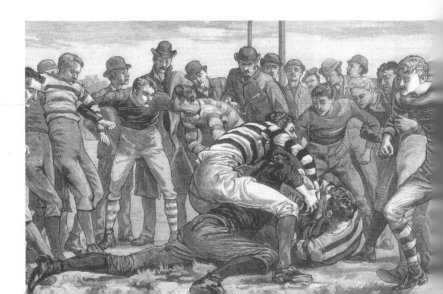

Splendid cathedrals

The cathedrals of Hereford, Worcester and Lichfield are fine examples of medieval architecture. Coventry Cathedral was bombed during World War II. A stunning new cathedral was built beside its ruins.

◄ **Coventry Cathedral**
St Michael's Cathedral, designed by architect Sir Basil Spence, was consecrated in 1962.

▼ **Penny Farthing**
James Starley of Coventry built this strange, early bicycle in 1870.

Industry

Birmingham has been nicknamed the 'city of 1,001 trades.' It is true that there are many successful industries there, particularly jewellery-making and other metalworking. Coventry was the birthplace of the bicycle and has a large car industry. It is also famous for its aircraft, which is why it suffered such heavy bombing during World War II. Leicester has shoe factories. Stoke-on-Trent is the centre of the ceramics industry. Wedgwood, Spode and Royal Doulton all have factories here. Together with nearby towns, it makes up an industrial area known as 'the Potteries.' Worcester and Derby are also known for their fine porcelain.

▼ **Early Wedgwood designs**

▼ **Supersonic car**
Record-breaking racer *Thrust 2* is housed at Coventry's Museum of British Road Transport.

▼ **Chocolate heaven**
Just outside Birmingham is Cadbury World, in the village of Bournville. Bournville was built to house workers at Cadbury's chocolate factory. About 800 bars come off the factory's conveyor belts every minute!

Farming

Market gardening and fruit farming are widespread across the fertile Vale of Evesham. Much of the produce is sold fresh from roadside stalls. Smallholdings produce a range of produce, including soft fruits, lettuces, broccoli, cauliflowers and asparagus. The Derbyshire Dales are known for their sheep farming.

► **Fresh produce**

East Midlands

▼ **The Fens**

MOST OF THE EAST MIDLANDS is low-lying and was at one time regularly flooded, partly by rivers and partly by the sea. During the 1600s, Dutch engineers drained large areas of the land.

The chalky Chiltern Hills lie along the southern boundary of this region. North from these, in Northamptonshire, lies the valley of the river Nene, running between two ridges of higher ground. In the southeast, Cambridgeshire is flat, broken only by the low Gog Magog Hills. The rest of this region is low-lying, much of it forming part of the fenland that still covers so much of eastern England. Further north, in Lincolnshire, the county consists of heathland, with wolds (low hills) to the east, and marshland over in the west running towards the North Sea. The river Trent, England's third-largest river, runs through Nottinghamshire to join the river Ouse and form the Humber. The whole fenland is criss-crossed by dozens of rivers and small streams. Sherwood Forest, associated forever with Robin Hood, lies in the north of Nottinghamshire.

▲ **Père David's deer**
Woburn Abbey is home to a herd of Père David's deer. This rare Chinese species was saved from extinction when it was bred here by the Duke of Bedford.

▲ **Punch and Judy**
Enjoy a traditional puppet show in the seaside town of Skegness, or 'Skeggy.'

▼ *Pilgrim's Progress*
The hero of Bunyan's tale, Christian, journeys from the City of Destruction to the Celestial City with a burden on his back. The story tells how he triumphs over evil.

Important towns

The region's most important cities and towns are the ancient ones of Bedford, Cambridge, Ely, Lincoln, Northampton, Nottingham and Peterborough. Bedford is famous as the home of the preacher John Bunyan. Grimsby in northeast Lincolnshire is a fishing port. The region has two major airports, Luton and East Midlands. There are five universities in the region: Bedford (Cranfield), Cambridge, Lincoln (Lincoln and Humberside, with its main campus in Hull) and Nottingham (two).

▲ **King's College**
Cambridge is home to England's second-oldest university. There are over 30 colleges, including King's, begun in 1446.

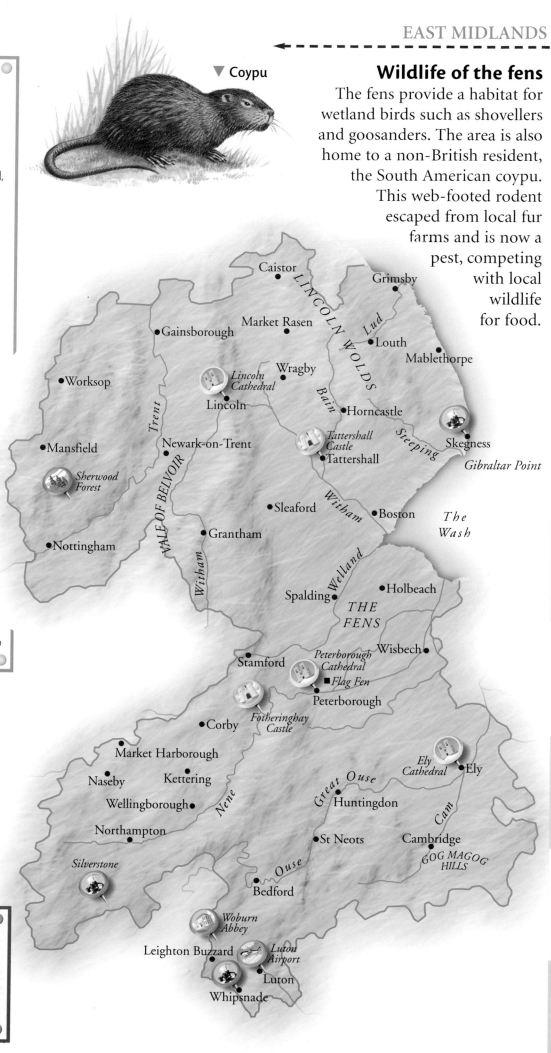

▼ Coypu

Wildlife of the fens

The fens provide a habitat for wetland birds such as shovellers and goosanders. The area is also home to a non-British resident, the South American coypu. This web-footed rodent escaped from local fur farms and is now a pest, competing with local wildlife for food.

GOOSE FAIR

Nottingham's famous Goose Fair has been held each October since the Middle Ages. Until the 1900s, thousands of geese would be herded by foot to the city. Mud 'socks' protected the birds' feet on their journey.

Caistor
Grimsby
Market Rasen
LINCOLN WOLDS
Lud
Louth
Mablethorpe
Gainsborough
Wragby
Bain
G
Worksop
Lincoln Cathedral
Lincoln
Horncastle
Steeping
Skegness
F
Mansfield
Trent
Newark-on-Trent
Tattershall Castle
Tattershall
Gibraltar Point
Sherwood Forest
VALE OF BELVOIR
Witham
Nottingham
Witham
Sleaford
Boston
The Wash
Grantham
Welland
Holbeach
E
Spalding
THE FENS
Wisbech
Stamford
Peterborough Cathedral
Flag Fen
D
Peterborough
Corby
Fotheringhay Castle
Market Harborough
Ely Cathedral
Ely
Naseby
Kettering
Great Ouse
Wellingborough
Nene
Huntingdon
Cam
C
Northampton
St Neots
Cambridge
Silverstone
GOG MAGOG HILLS
Ouse
B
Bedford
Woburn Abbey
Leighton Buzzard
Luton Airport
Luton
A
Whipsnade

▲ Roman soldiers
The Ermine Street Guard dress up in perfect replicas of ancient Roman uniforms and weapons.

▼ Oliver Cromwell

▼ The Battle of Naseby
On June 14, 1645 Charles I and his Royalist army were defeated by Cromwell's troops. The victors were known as Roundheads because of their pudding-bowl haircuts.

STONE AGE PEOPLE lived in much of the region, and they have left behind earthworks and trackways. The waterlogged ground has preserved ancient timbers from pre-Roman times, notably at Flag Fen, near Peterborough.

The Romans worked their way north through this region, building a network of roads, many of which are important routes today. Among them was Ermine Street, linking *Londinium* (London) with *Ledum* (Lincoln). The Anglo Saxons arrived in the AD400s, founding many of the present-day towns and villages. They were followed by the Vikings, who invaded in the 800s.

On the battlefield

Northampton was one of the many places where battles were fought during the Wars of the Roses in the 1400s. One of the deciding battles of the English Civil War was at Naseby, Northamptonshire. Here, Parliamentary general Oliver Cromwell and his New Model Army defeated the Royalist army of Charles I in 1646.

Castles

There are several castles in the region, and a few are partly intact, such as Tattershall in Lincolnshire, built of red brick in the 1400s. The great tower survives, standing 33 metres high. Only the foundations remain of Fotheringhay, Northamptonshire, where Mary, Queen of Scots, was imprisoned and later executed.

CATHEDRALS

ELY, CAMBRIDGESHIRE
Saxon queen Etheldreda founded an abbey on this site in AD673. The Norman cathedral was finished in 1189. Its octagonal tower was added in 1322.

PETERBOROUGH, CAMBRIDGESHIRE
Henry VIII's first wife, Catherine of Aragon, was buried in this Norman cathedral in 1536. The nave has a beautifully-painted timber ceiling.

LINCOLN, LINCOLNSHIRE
Built in the Middle Ages, this cathedral has three tall towers. The central one is over 80 metres high, but was twice that until it toppled in a storm in 1547.

▲ The Great Tower
All that remains of Tattershall Castle, Lincolnshire, are its red-brick tower and moats. Peacocks strut about the scenic grounds and there is also a guardhouse museum.

◀ **Lincoln Museum of Life**
Here, visitors learn about the region's traditional crafts and skills, such as cheese-making.

ROBIN HOOD
Legendary outlaw Robin Hood is said to have lived in Sherwood Forest during the reign of Richard I. Robin Hood was loyal to the king and opposed to his wicked brother John. Along with his Merry Men, he stole from the rich and gave to the poor.

Industry
Nottingham has a worldwide reputation for its fine lace. There are also heavy industries and many power stations along the banks of the river Trent. Northampton is an important leatherworking centre. The clay beds of Bedfordshire have been quarried for brickmaking. Precision instruments are made around Cambridge.

Farming and fishing
The rich, peaty fens have made the East Midlands one of England's most important arable lands. The region's farmers supply fruit and vegetables to local industries for freezing, canning and jam-making. Other crops include cereals and sugarbeet. Shorthorn cows provide milk for making Stilton cheese, in Nottinghamshire.

▲ **Doc Martens**
The first of these workmen's boots was made in 1960 in Northampton. Its unique air-cushioned sole was designed by two foot specialists, Dr Maerten and Dr Funck.

▼ **Silverstone**
The British Grand Prix is held each July at Silverstone race track in Northamptonshire.

◀ Sugarbeet

CAN YOU FIND?
1 Ely Cathedral
2 Sherwood Forest
3 Silverstone
4 Tattershall Castle
5 Wisbech

see page 31

East Anglia

EAST ANGLIA IS MADE UP OF the counties of Norfolk and Suffolk. It is named after the Angles, a Germanic tribe from Angeln in Schleswig, southern Denmark, who invaded England in the AD400s.

The counties of Norfolk and Suffolk form a bulge on the east coast of England. They have a long coastline, extending from the Wash in the northwest to the Essex border in the south. The Wash is a large, square bay between Norfolk and Lincolnshire. There are low hills in the northern part of Norfolk, but the county is otherwise very flat, with some land lying below sea level. The Little Ouse and river Nen form the western boundary with Cambridgeshire. Here the land is part of the fenland that extends up into Lincolnshire. The Little Ouse and the river Waveney form the boundary with Suffolk. Most of Suffolk is gently undulating country, with the eastern end of the Chiltern Hills in the southwest. The river Stour separates Suffolk from Essex.

Important towns

Norwich is the chief city of Norfolk. It has a fine Norman cathedral and castle and is also home to the region's only university, East Anglia. Ipswich, at the head of the river Orwell's estuary, is Suffolk's chief town. Great Yarmouth, Norfolk, is a holiday resort and a port. It supplies the North Sea oil industry and handles freight from continental Europe. Just across the county border, Lowestoft is another resort and fishing port. In the west, Newmarket attracts horse-dealers to its annual auction. The town has two famous racecourses and, in 1967, the Queen opened the National Stud there.

▼ **Spooky owl**
On a clear night you might see a barn owl, scanning the land for prey, such as mice or shrews.

▼ **Along the coast**
The harbours at Lowestoft, Cromer and King's Lynn are crowded with fishing boats.

▲ **Timber town**
Lavenham in Suffolk has over 300 listed buildings. From the Middle Ages until the late 1500s, the village was an important centre of the wool trade.

▼ **Patchwork traders**
Norwich's large market is one of Britain's oldest – it has stood on the same site outside the guildhall for over 900 years. Its colourful stall awnings are known as tilts.

COUNTY FACTS

NORFOLK
Area: 5,335 sq km
Population: 772,400
Administrative centre: Norwich
Other key places: Great Yarmouth, King's Lynn

SUFFOLK
Area: 3,800 sq km
Population: 379,700
Administrative centre: Ipswich
Other key places: Felixstowe, Lowestoft, Newmarket

The Broads

The East Anglian landscape is dominated by the Broads, a series of shallow lakes near the coast, all interlinked by natural waterways. Some of the lakes were formed by holes left by digging up peat in the Middle Ages. Today, the Broads are a popular destination for holidaymakers and wildlife watchers.

NORTH SEA

Scolt Head — Blakeney Point
Hunstanton — Wells-next-the-Sea — Cromer
The Wash
Little Walsingham
Sandringham House — Fakenham
Bure
Wensum
Hoveton
Nene — Great Ouse — King's Lynn
Dereham — Norwich Cathedral — THE BROADS
FENLAND — Swaffham — Yare — Norwich — Yare — Great Yarmouth
Downham Market
Wissey
Little Ouse — Thet — Waveney — Lowestoft
Thetford — Diss — Beccles
Lark — Southwold
Newmarket — Bury St Edmunds — Framlingham Castle
Gripping — Framlingham — Saxmundham
Stowmarket — Burgh Castle — Aldeburgh
Lavenham — Burgh — Orford Castle — Orford
Woodbridge — Orford Ness
Sudbury — Ipswich — Sutton
Stour — Felixstowe

▲ **House on stilts**
This water tower was built in the 1920s to serve the holiday town of Thorpeness, Suffolk. It is known as the House in the Clouds and includes a five-storey house.

◀ **Return of the otter**
Once hunted for fur and threatened by pollution, otters have now been reintroduced into a reserve beside the river Waveney, in Suffolk.

CLASSIC BUILDING
The University of East Anglia is a mecca for lovers of modern architecture. A cluster of stepped pyramids built in 1968 houses the students, while architect Norman Foster's Sainsbury Centre contains a priceless collection of art.

F
E
D
C
B
A

▲ Ancient helmet
Anglo-Saxon artefacts buried in a ship at Sutton Hoo near Woodbridge, Suffolk, date back to AD620. Archaeologists found the treasures in 1939.

D URING THE STONE AGE Norfolk was the centre of a major flint industry. Grimes Graves, near Thetford, was the biggest flint mine in Europe. There were hundreds of mine shafts, some up to 12 metres deep, when the mine was in use between 2600BC and 1200BC.

Further south, the ancient British tribe of the Iceni flourished in Suffolk. After the Romans occupied the country, Boudicca, a queen of the Iceni, led a revolt against them, which was crushed. The Anglo Saxons established the kingdom of East Anglia in the AD500s. Its capital was at Dunwich, but the sea swallowed up its palaces centuries ago. Today Dunwich is a small, ordinary coastal village.

Vikings and kings
The Vikings conquered the area in the late 800s, and many place names show their influence to this day. Bury St Edmunds gets its name from the fact that King Edmund of East Anglia was buried there after he was murdered by the Vikings in 870. Another local legend tells how King John lost his baggage, including treasure, and part of his army to the tide while trying to take a short cut across the sands of the Wash in 1216.

Place of pilgrimage
In the Middle Ages, people flocked from all over Europe to the shrine at Walsingham in north Norfolk. Pilgrimages lapsed after the Reformation in the 1500s, until a new shrine was erected in the 1920s.

▲ Vision of a virgin
The Shrine of Our Lady at Walsingham was erected by Richeldis, Lady of the Manor, in 1061. She said that the Virgin Mary had appeared to her there.

◀ Digging for flint
Neolithic miners used antler picks or stone axes to dig the hard, shiny flint from the surrounding chalk. Flint was used for axe-heads and other tools.

▲ *Flatford Mill* by John Constable

HAUNTED HOUSE

Norfolk's Blickling Hall was once home to Anne Boleyn, second wife of Henry VIII. On the anniversary of her execution, a horse-drawn coach is said to drive the queen up to the house. Spookily, the horses, coachmen and their royal passenger are all headless!

Castles and country houses

Burgh Castle, near Great Yarmouth, was the largest Roman fort in the region. Three of its walls are still standing. Most of the medieval castles in East Anglia are in ruins, but the Great Tower of Orford Castle still stands, a reminder of the time when it was the most important castle in the area. Towers and a mighty wall remain of Framlingham Castle, where Queen Mary I sheltered while rebels tried to put her second cousin, Lady Jane Grey, on the throne. The most important of the great houses that survive is Sandringham House, the Queen's country residence. Members of the Royal Family holiday there.

Industry

Fishing is the region's most important industry. Cod, herring and flatfish are brought into Lowestoft, while at King's Lynn, situated on the relatively shallow bay of the Wash, the boats trawl for shellfish. Cromer is famous for its crabs. The Norfolk village of Orford is known for its smokehouses, where meats and fish are preserved.

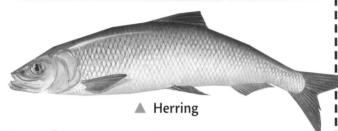

▲ Herring

Farming

East Anglia is a great agricultural region. Farmers grow cereals, sugarbeet, fruit and vegetables, and they raise turkeys, sheep and cattle. Red Polls are a breed of cattle that originated here. They are stocky, with no horns, and are kept for both milk and beef. Suffolk Punches are a breed of large, chestnut-coloured draught horses.

▶ Suffolk Punch

CAN YOU FIND?

1 Bury St Edmunds
2 Great Yarmouth
3 Lavenham
4 Sandringham House
5 Little Walsingham

see page 35

◀ **Brewers of Bury St Edmunds**
Greene King has made beer since 1799, using mineral-rich water drawn from a well beneath the brewery.

The Northwest

THE NORTHWEST INCLUDES one of England's main centres of industry. The region became famous in the 18th century for spinning and weaving, and cotton mills and factories dotted the Lancashire landscape.

Northwest England consists of the two counties of Lancashire and Cheshire, together with the former metropolitan counties of Greater Manchester and Merseyside. There is a wide, fertile plain in the west, sloping up to the Pennine Hills in the east. These hills trap the rain-bearing clouds that blow in from the Irish Sea, giving the region a moist climate. The northeastern part of the region, which lies to the east of the M6 motorway, is an area of wide-open spaces, including Bleasdale Moor and the Forest of Bowland. The forest is designated as an Area of Outstanding Natural Beauty. The region's main rivers are the Lune in the north, the Ribble and, in the south, the river Mersey, which forms a large part of the boundary between Lancashire and Cheshire. To the west, Lancashire has a long coastline, and some of the land bordering the sea is reclaimed marshland. Further south, Cheshire's only sea coast is on the Wirral Peninsula, which lies between the wide estuaries of the Mersey and the Dee.

Important towns

Manchester and Liverpool are the Northwest's largest cities and both are important ports. Liverpool, Britain's second-largest port after London, was for many years the main British terminal for transatlantic liners. The port of Manchester lies 58 kilometres inland but is connected to the sea by the Manchester Ship Canal. Manchester and Liverpool both have busy airports. Chester is Cheshire's chief town. Roman-built walls surround the city and its beautiful cathedral. The region has seven universities at Lancaster, Liverpool (two), Manchester (two), Preston and Salford.

▼ **Blackpool Illuminations**
The seaside resort of Blackpool puts on a dazzling display of lights for its summer visitors. The 150-metre-high tower dates back to 1894.

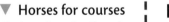

▼ **Horses for courses**
Each spring, the Grand National steeplechase is held at Aintree, Liverpool. The racetrack includes 31 tricky jumps.

▲ **Martin Mere**
This Lancashire nature reserve is home to rare birds, such as the pink-footed goose.

▼ **Heather**
Beautiful heathers bloom on Bleasdale Moor.

COUNTY FACTS

CHESHIRE
Area: 2,330 sq km
Population: 978,100
Administrative centre: Chester
Other key places: Crewe, Warrington

GREATER MANCHESTER
Area: 1,285 sq km
Population: 2,583,000
Administrative centre: Manchester
Other key places: Wigan

LANCASHIRE
Area: 3,070 sq km
Population: 1,426,000
Administrative centre: Preston
Other key places: Blackburn, Blackpool, Lancaster

MERSEYSIDE
Area: 640 sq km
Population: 1,481,000
Administrative centre: Liverpool
Other key places: Prescot

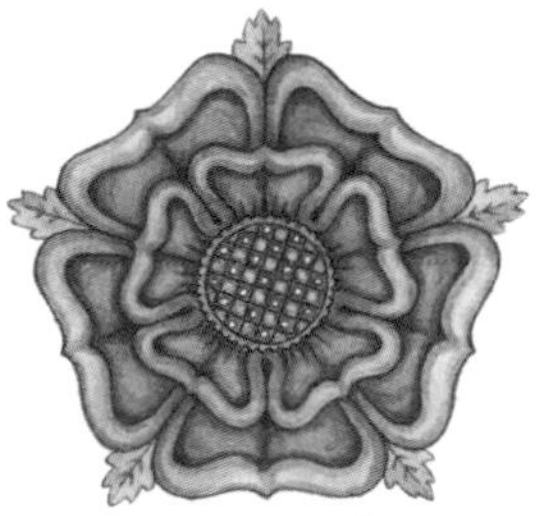

▲ **Red rose of Lancaster**

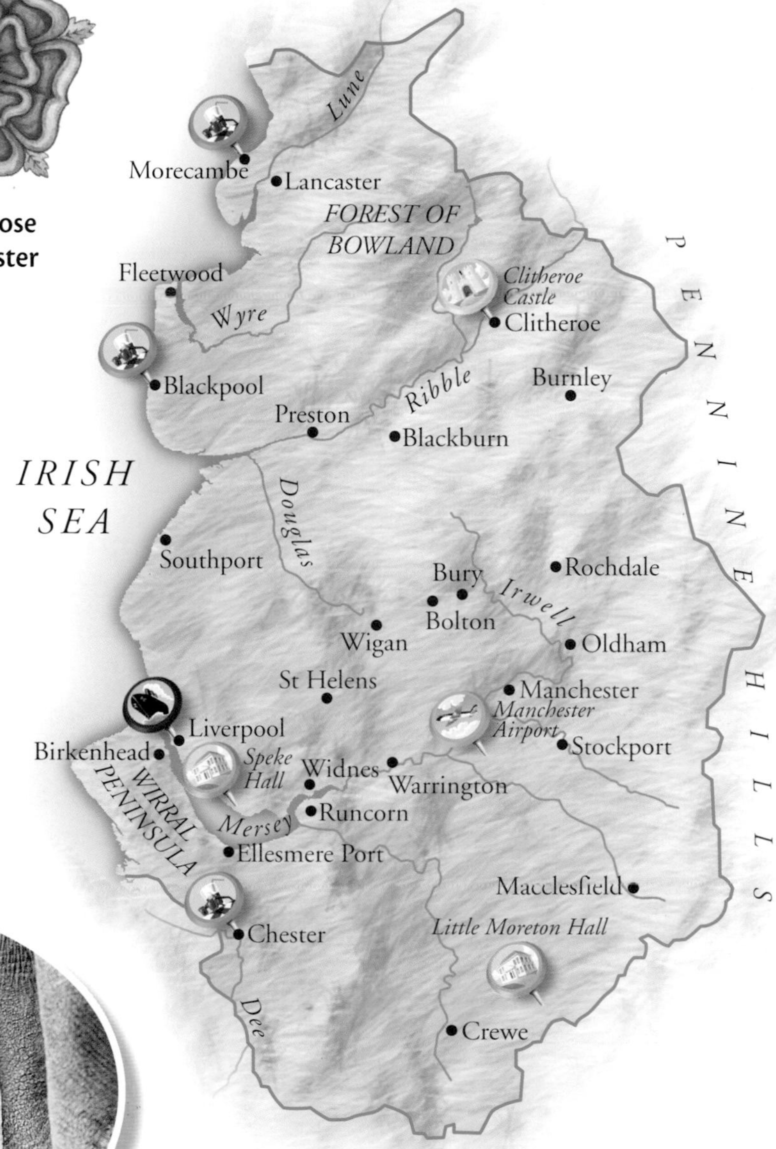
Lune
Morecambe
Lancaster
FOREST OF BOWLAND
Fleetwood
Wyre
Clitheroe Castle
Clitheroe
PENNINE HILLS
Blackpool
Ribble
Burnley
Preston
Blackburn
IRISH SEA
Douglas
Southport
Bury
Rochdale
Irwell
Bolton
Wigan
Oldham
St Helens
Manchester
Manchester Airport
Liverpool
Birkenhead
Stockport
Speke Hall
Widnes
Warrington
WIRRAL PENINSULA
Mersey
Runcorn
Ellesmere Port
Macclesfield
Chester
Little Moreton Hall
Dee
Crewe

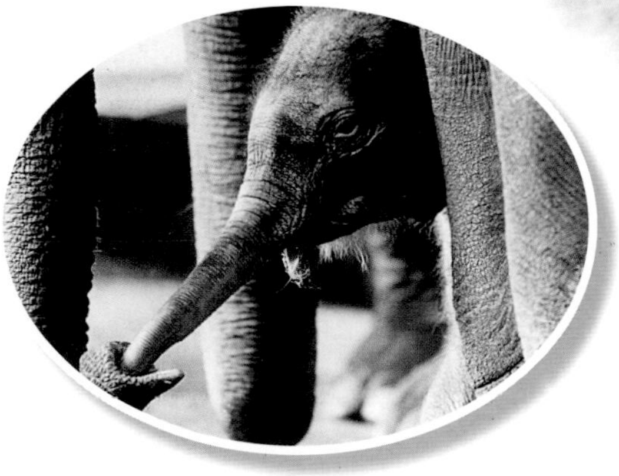

▶ **Chester's attractions**
Visitors to Chester, a historic, walled town built by the Romans, can enjoy a trip to England's largest zoo.

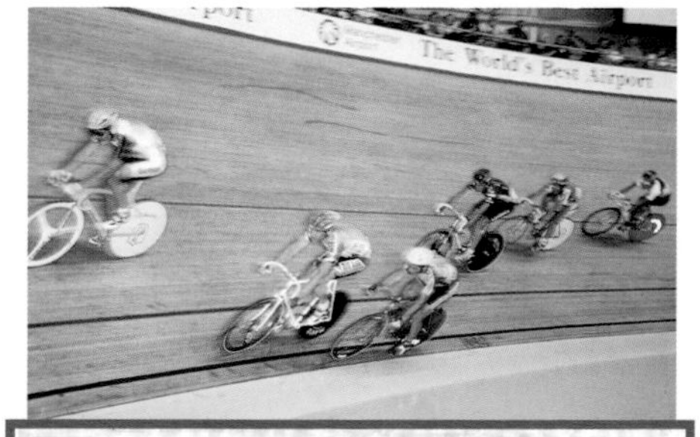
The World's Best Airport

PURPOSE-BUILT

The country's first indoor cycle-racing track, or velodrome, opened in Manchester in 1994. The domed structure is constructed from 600 tonnes of steel.

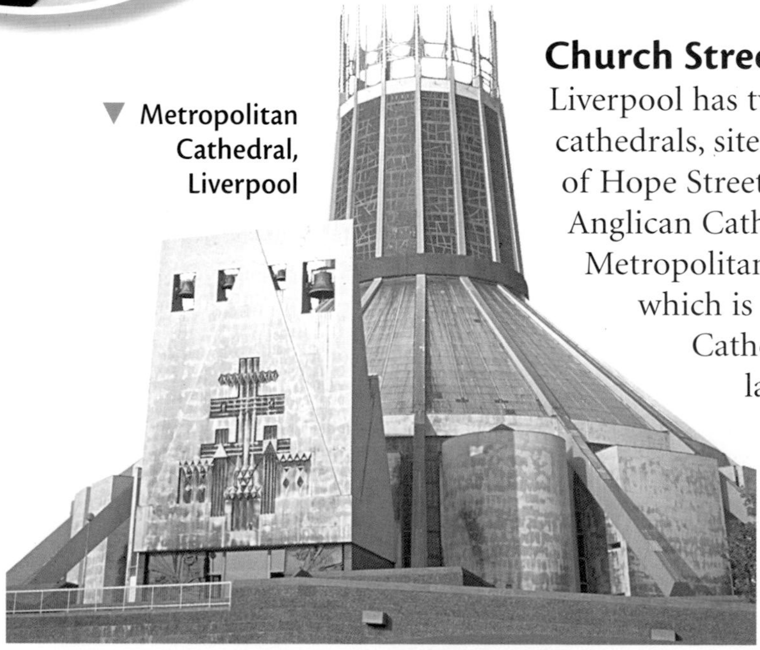

▼ **Metropolitan Cathedral, Liverpool**

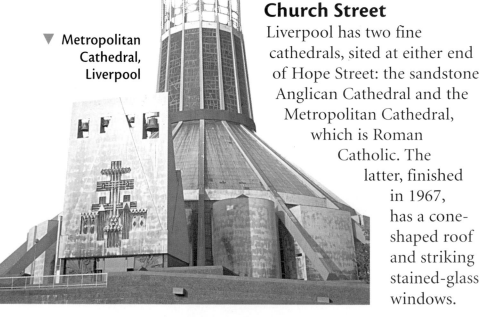

Church Street

Liverpool has two fine cathedrals, sited at either end of Hope Street: the sandstone Anglican Cathedral and the Metropolitan Cathedral, which is Roman Catholic. The latter, finished in 1967, has a cone-shaped roof and striking stained-glass windows.

THERE ARE TRACES OF STONE AGE SETTLEMENTS in the region, including a stone circle in Cheshire. There are also remains of Bronze and Iron Age peoples.

In Roman times an important fort was built at *Deva* (modern Chester). A road connected it with forts at Manchester and Lancaster, and a settlement at *Coccium* (Wigan). Other roads led up to Hadrian's Wall. The finest example of a Roman road to be seen in England is at Blackstone Edge, near Littleborough.

Anglo Saxons, Vikings and Normans

The Anglo Saxons settled the Northwest later than other regions of England. As a result, they were soon dispossessed by the Vikings. The first Norman castle was built at Lancaster by Roger of Poitou, one of William the Conqueror's noblemen. The earls of Chester ruled Cheshire after the Norman conquest. In 1241 Henry III made Chester a 'county palatine,' giving its lord special powers, such as his own parliament. Lancashire was also given this status, in 1351.

Growth of trade

From the late 1600s Liverpool's development was based on the sugarcane trade from the West Indies, and on the slave trade from Africa. With the arrival of steam power in the mid-19th century, the port grew rapidly. Thousands of Irish refugees sailed into Liverpool during the Potato Famine of the 1840s. Manchester's growth began in earnest during the Industrial Revolution.

▲ **Earl of Chester**
Since the mid-1300s, the earldom of Chester has been one of the titles held by the princes of Wales.

▼ **There was a crooked house...**
Little Moreton Hall, near Crewe, Cheshire, is an amazing half-timbered house dating back to Tudor times.

IN A SPIN
English weaver and carpenter James Hargreaves invented the spinning jenny in about 1764. The machine could spin more than one thread at once and sped up the cloth-making process.

▲ **Down at the docks**
Liverpool's shipbuilding declined in the 1980s but Albert Dock was redeveloped to attract tourism.

CAN YOU FIND?

1 Blackpool
2 Chester
3 Forest of Bowland
4 Little Moreton Hall
5 Manchester
6 Morecambe

see page 39

THE CHESHIRE CAT

The much-loved story of *Alice's Adventures in Wonderland* (1865) was written by Cheshire-born Lewis Carroll, whose real name was Charles Dodgson. One of his characters is the Cheshire Cat, a feline with the magical ability to make its whole body disappear – except for its wide, cheeky grin!

Canals and railways

England's first canal opened in 1761 to carry coal from the Duke of Bridgewater's estate at Worsley to nearby Manchester. It was the first of a whole network. The Manchester Ship Canal opened in 1894. The world's first successful commercial rail track, the Liverpool-to-Manchester railway, had opened in 1830.

▲ Building the Manchester Ship Canal

Industry

The Industrial Revolution developed round Manchester. As the cotton trade grew, mill towns replaced ancient villages. Modern Manchester's industries include clothing, banking and manufacturing. Its Granada Studios create television shows including the long-running soap opera, *Coronation Street*. Granada also have studios in Albert Dock, Liverpool. Liverpool has flour mills, sugar refineries, car plants and a few remaining shipyards. Cheshire's fortunes were founded on salt deposits; today it has chemical industries.

Farming

Much of the region is rich farmland. Dairy cattle graze on the low plains between the Pennines and the hills of North Wales. Their milk is made into crumbly Cheshire or Lancashire cheese.

▲ **The Liver Birds**

Perched on top of the Royal Liver Building, Liverpool are two bronze birds. According to one legend, the birds lived by the muddy creek, or *lifrugpool*, where the city was founded in the 1st century AD.

▶ **Rocket racer**

George Stephenson built the Liverpool-to-Manchester railway. In 1830 his *Rocket* steam engine was first to travel the route – at a top speed of 58 km/h!

▶ **The Fab Four**

Liverpool was the birthplace of the biggest pop band ever. The Beatles – John, Paul, George and Ringo – were chart-toppers in the 1960s.

▶ **Football crazy**

Top football teams Manchester United and Liverpool are long-standing rivals – and so are their fans. Here, Manchester forward Dwight Yorke (in blue) takes on Liverpool's Steve Gerrard (in red).

The Northeast

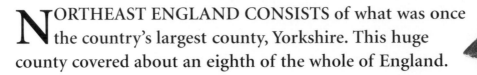

▼ Robin Hood's Bay
is a tiny seaside village between Scarborough and Whitby. This stretch of coast was once a famous haunt of smugglers.

NORTHEAST ENGLAND CONSISTS of what was once the country's largest county, Yorkshire. This huge county covered about an eighth of the whole of England.

The landscape of the Northeast is very varied. In the west are the Pennines and their foothills, which are divided by the Dales, long valleys that run from east to west. The highest Pennine peak in Yorkshire is Cross Fell (790 metres). Fast-flowing rivers, fed by numerous moorland streams, pass through the Dales and join the river Humber. The area boasts spectacular waterfalls and a scenic limestone landscape around Malham. East of the Pennines are the Central Lowlands and, farther east still, the higher ground of the Cleveland Hills, the North York Moors and the Yorkshire Wolds. The Wolds join the sea as cliffs at Flamborough Head. Farther south, the long Holderness Peninsula is low-lying and is constantly being eroded by the waves. Both the Dales and the North York Moors are National Parks.

▲ Red grouse
This moorland bird feeds on young shoots of heather and sweet, wild bilberries.

Important towns

In the southwest lies an industrial belt of large manufacturing cities and towns. In descending order of size they include Sheffield, Leeds, Bradford, Huddersfield, Doncaster, Rotherham and Halifax. There is an international airport between Leeds and Bradford. Kingston-upon-Hull, generally known as Hull, is a ferry, container and fishing port, with many industries. The historic city of York is a popular tourist attraction. Harrogate rose to prominence as a spa town in the 1800s and has over 80 mineral springs. The Northeast has nine universities, at Bradford, Huddersfield, Hull (two, including the University of Lincoln and Humberside), Leeds (two), Sheffield (two) and York.

▼ Eureka! Museum
This brilliant museum near Bradford teaches young children about science – without their realizing it!

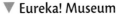

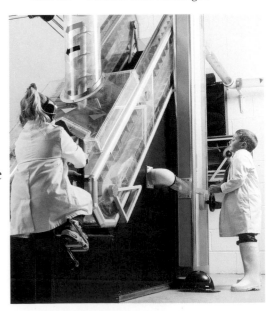

▼ Bat and ball
The home ground of the world-renowned Yorkshire County Cricket Club is at Headingley, just outside Leeds.

BRILLIANT BRIDGE

Spanning the 1,410-metre-wide river Humber just outside Hull is the magnificent Humber Suspension Bridge, completed in 1981. The bridge's towers rise over 150 metres above their supports.

◄ **White rose of York**

Cathedral city

The War of the Roses was a fight for the English throne between the Houses of York (whose emblem was a white rose) and Lancaster (represented by a red rose). York Minster's Rose Window combines both roses.

▶ **The Rose Window, York Minster**

COUNTY FACTS

EAST RIDING OF YORKSHIRE
Area: 3,035 sq km
Population: 308,400
Key places: Beverley, Bridlington, Goole, Kingston-upon-Hull

NORTH YORKSHIRE
Area: 8,310 sq km
Population: 556,200
Administrative centre: Northallerton
Other key places: Harrogate, Ripon, Scarborough, Whitby, York

SOUTH YORKSHIRE
Area: 1,560 sq km
Population: 1,303,200
Key places: Barnsley, Doncaster, Rotherham, Sheffield

WEST YORKSHIRE
Area: 2,040 sq km
Population: 2,052,800
Key places: Bradford, Halifax, Huddersfield, Leeds, Wakefield

YORKSHIRE HAS MANY STONE AGE REMAINS, some dating back to 8000BC. There are several hill forts, including Dane's Dyke near Flamborough Head.

The Brigantes, an ancient British tribe that occupied the region during the Iron Age, built a fortification at Stanwick, near Richmond, as a defence against the Romans. The Romans built forts at *Eboracum* (York), *Cataractonium* (Catterick – an army base even today), *Danum* (Doncaster) and at least 20 other places. They also mined lead in the Pennines. In AD306 the Roman general Constantine was proclaimed emperor of Rome at York.

▲ **Henry Moore**
Twentieth-century sculptor Henry Moore went to art college in Leeds. The city now has a museum dedicated to the artist.

▶ **Famous explorer**
In 1728 Captain James Cook was born at Marton-in-Cleveland. Later famous for exploring the Americas and Australasia, the young Cook did his seaman's apprenticeship at nearby Whitby.

◀ ▼ **Castle Howard**
This stunning stately home, just outside York, is a firm favourite with film directors. It was the setting for the 1982 TV series *Brideshead Revisited*.

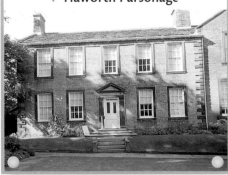

THE BRONTËS
The village of Haworth, West Yorkshire, was the childhood home of three talented writers – the Brontë sisters. The girls' mother died when they were young and they were educated at home by their father, an Irish curate.

ANNE BRONTË (1820–49)
Author of *Agnes Grey* and *The Tenant of Wildfell Hall*

CHARLOTTE BRONTË (1816–55)
Author of *Jane Eyre* and *Villette*

EMILY JANE BRONTË (1818–48)
Author of *Wuthering Heights*

▼ **Haworth Parsonage**

Anglo Saxons, Vikings and Normans
The Anglo Saxons moved into the area in the 500s, after the Romans left. By the 700s their kingdom of Northumbria extended from the Humber up to the Forth. It was an important Christian centre, strongly influenced by Ireland's Celtic Church. The Vikings occupied Yorkshire in 867. When the Normans arrived, they met stiff resistance. To crush any opposition, William the Conqueror razed a large area to the ground, in what became known as 'the harrying of the North.' The Normans built strategic castles from which they could control the region, including Conisbrough Castle in South Yorkshire and Richmond Castle, near Catterick. The original timber castle in York stood until 1228, when it was replaced by a stone tower.

▲ Pit ponies

Miners used pony power to pull coal to the surface until the advent of steam engines.

Religious riches

York Minster is one of the country's finest cathedrals, with magnificent stained-glass windows. Beverley Minster and Selby Abbey are beautiful, too. There are remains of several monasteries, which were dissolved by Henry VIII. These include Fountains Abbey, Rievaulx Abbey and Byland Abbey, all in North Yorkshire.

◀ Dry stone wall

Industry

Engineering and textiles are the region's two top industries, and are concentrated in West and South Yorkshire. Sheffield's silver and steel industries have a worldwide name. A Sheffield-made knife was even mentioned in Chaucer's *Canterbury Tales*. For many years Yorkshire's coalfields provided much of the fuel used in British industry, but most mines have now closed. Leeds-based crafts included handmade tintacks and smoking pipes cast in clay.

▲ Moorland sheep

Farming

Dairy farmers in the Dales make delicious cheeses, such as Wensleydale and Swaledale. The moors provide rough grazing for sheep. The lambs are born in the sheltered valleys and moved up into hills until the autumn, when the moors become bleak and snow-covered.

▲ Stainless steel

One of the top cutlery designers based around Sheffield is David Mellor. His unusual, circular factory at the nearby village of Hathersage was built in 1988.

CAN YOU FIND?

1 Castle Howard	4 Sheffield
2 Conisbrough Castle	5 York
3 Halifax	Minster

see page 43

The North

▼ **Cockleybeck**
This small, picturesque river flows through Cumbria's National Park.

▼ **God of the Tyne**
This sculpture in Newcastle celebrates the river Tyne. The city has six famous bridges spanning the river, including a combined road and rail bridge designed by Robert Stephenson.

THE NORTH OF ENGLAND is often called the 'Border Country' because it is on the frontier with Scotland. For hundreds of years people from both sides of the border used to raid each other's territory, sometimes fighting fierce battles, but often just stealing cattle or sheep.

To the east of the region is Cumbria. It is known as the Lake District because it contains 15 large lakes, the biggest of which is Windermere. The county also has England's biggest mountains – Scafell Pike (978 metres) is the highest peak. Most of the Lake District is a National Park, attracting tourists, climbers, hillwalkers and water sports enthusiasts. Much of Northumberland, too, forms a National Park, offering remote fell walks and some of England's most dramatic scenery. About 56 kilometres of the border with Scotland is formed by the Cheviot Hills. Nearby lies Kielder Water, one of the largest man-made lakes in northern Europe. In southern Northumberland is the start of the Pennine Hills, England's 'backbone.' To the south is the low-lying county of Tyne and Wear. Durham is partly in the Pennines and partly coastal lowland. The region's main rivers are the Tyne and the Wear in the east, and the Derwent and the Eden in the west.

Important towns
The largest urban areas are in the east. Newcastle-upon-Tyne is the biggest city; others include historic Berwick-upon-Tweed and the cathedral city of Durham. Important towns include Sunderland, Tynemouth, Gateshead and Stockton-on-Tees. To the west lie the border city of Carlisle and industrial Barrow-in-Furness, part of Lancashire until 1974. The region has five universities, at Durham (the third-oldest in England), Middlesbrough, Newcastle-upon-Tyne (two), and Sunderland.

▼ **Poetic landscape**
William Wordsworth's romantic lyrics captured the beauty of the Lake District. He famously described the 'host of golden daffodils' that flower on the hillsides there each spring.

▼ **Windsurfing on Lake Windermere**

▶ **Angel of the A1**
Gateshead, Tyne and Wear, is home to the Angel of the North. Built by sculptor Antony Gormley in 1998, it stands nearly 20 metres high and has a wingspan of more than 50 metres.

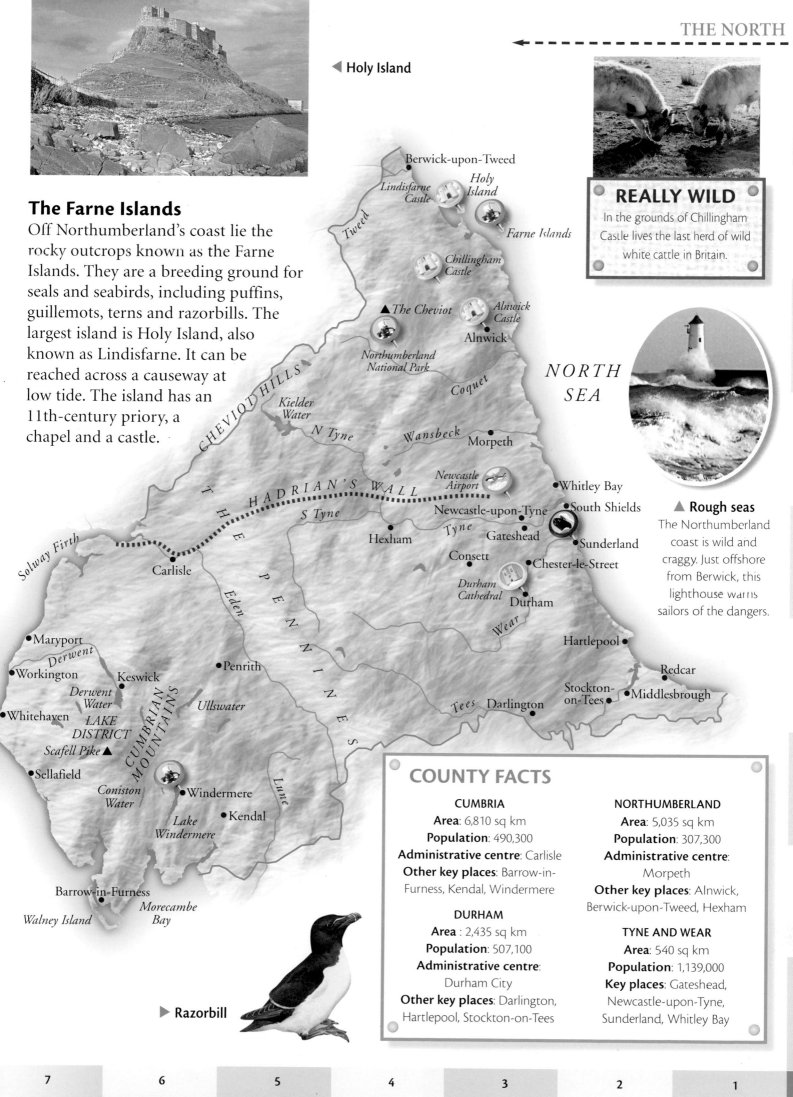

◀ Holy Island

The Farne Islands

Off Northumberland's coast lie the rocky outcrops known as the Farne Islands. They are a breeding ground for seals and seabirds, including puffins, guillemots, terns and razorbills. The largest island is Holy Island, also known as Lindisfarne. It can be reached across a causeway at low tide. The island has an 11th-century priory, a chapel and a castle.

REALLY WILD

In the grounds of Chillingham Castle lives the last herd of wild white cattle in Britain.

▲ **Rough seas**

The Northumberland coast is wild and craggy. Just offshore from Berwick, this lighthouse warns sailors of the dangers.

Berwick-upon-Tweed
Lindisfarne Castle
Holy Island
Farne Islands
Tweed
Chillingham Castle
▲ The Cheviot
Alnwick Castle
Alnwick
Northumberland National Park
Kielder Water
Coquet

NORTH SEA

CHEVIOT HILLS
N Tyne
Wansbeck
Morpeth
HADRIAN'S WALL
Newcastle Airport
Whitley Bay
Newcastle-upon-Tyne
South Shields
S Tyne
Tyne
Gateshead
Hexham
Sunderland
Consett
Chester-le-Street
Durham Cathedral
Durham
Wear

Solway Firth
Carlisle
Eden
THE PENNINES
Hartlepool
Maryport
Derwent
Penrith
Redcar
Workington
Keswick
Stockton-on-Tees
Middlesbrough
Derwent Water
Ullswater
Tees
Darlington
Whitehaven
LAKE DISTRICT
CUMBRIAN MOUNTAINS
Scafell Pike ▲
Sellafield
Coniston Water
Windermere
Lune
Lake Windermere
Kendal
Barrow-in-Furness
Morecambe Bay
Walney Island

▶ Razorbill

COUNTY FACTS

CUMBRIA
Area: 6,810 sq km
Population: 490,300
Administrative centre: Carlisle
Other key places: Barrow-in-Furness, Kendal, Windermere

DURHAM
Area : 2,435 sq km
Population: 507,100
Administrative centre: Durham City
Other key places: Darlington, Hartlepool, Stockton-on-Tees

NORTHUMBERLAND
Area: 5,035 sq km
Population: 307,300
Administrative centre: Morpeth
Other key places: Alnwick, Berwick-upon-Tweed, Hexham

TYNE AND WEAR
Area: 540 sq km
Population: 1,139,000
Key places: Gateshead, Newcastle-upon-Tyne, Sunderland, Whitley Bay

▲ **Fleeing the Vikings**
Monks carried treasures to
Durham for safety in AD995.
These included the illuminated
Lindisfarne Gospels.

T HERE ARE A FEW REMAINS of
Bronze Age people in the North,
but the earliest substantial remains
are from Roman times.

The Romans occupied the area from
AD80, building roads and numerous forts.
Their greatest achievement was the
construction of Hadrian's Wall, on the
orders of Emperor Hadrian who visited
the region in AD122.

Troubled times

Anglo Saxons settled in the area from the
5th century onwards. In the 9th century
the Vikings occupied northern England. Fear of these raiders
led the monks of Lindisfarne to found a church at Durham
in 995. The Normans took over after the Conquest in 1066,
but the region remained thinly-populated for a long time.
The Scots frequently invaded northern England: Cumbria,
for example, passed to and from English and Scottish rule
between 945 and 1157. As late as 1644 Newcastle was
captured by the Scots during the English Civil War.

HADRIAN'S WALL

Hadrian's Wall extends from the
Solway Firth in the west to the mouth
of the Tyne in the east, a distance
of 117 kilometres. It marked the
northernmost border of the Roman
Empire. The wall was nearly five metres
high. In places it ran along the edges of
cliffs or escarpments, but mostly it was
defended by wide, deep ditches.
Many stretches of the wall survive
almost intact, and the ruins of several
forts and camps have been excavated.
The Romans built small forts every
1,480 metres, as well as 16 larger forts
to house legions of soldiers. The
best-known fort is Housesteads.

▼ **Housesteads
Roman Fort**

▲ **Men dressed as Roman soldiers, Hadrian's Wall**

Castles and towers

The Normans built castles in order to keep control of
the territory. Part of Durham Castle is now used by
the university, which also uses the 14th-century
Lumley Castle in nearby Chester-le-Street. The keep
of Newcastle-upon-Tyne's castle, built in 1177,
still stands, and Carlisle Castle is in regular use. The
magnificent coastal castle at Bamburgh,
Northumberland, has been restored, and so has that
at Alnwick. Only the gatehouse tower at Hylton
Castle, in Tyne and Wear, still survives. Sizergh
Castle, near Kendal, is a pele tower (a simple fortified
residence), which was built in the 1300s by the
Strickland family who still occupy it. Pele towers
were common in northern England. There are several
in Northumberland, at Corbridge,
Chipchase and Belsay.

▼ **Bamburgh Castle**

THE LAMBTON WORM

According to legend, during the 1300s a monster worm terrorized County Durham, devouring children and cattle. After taking advice from a local witch, Sir John Lambton killed the worm, but because he didn't kill the very next person he saw as the witch instructed, he brought down a witch's curse on his family. Nine heads of the family died spooky deaths, the last in 1761.

Industry

From medieval times Cumbria and Northumberland mined iron ore, lead and silver. This mining, and coal production in the Whitehaven area, have now stopped, but some steel is still made in the Furness area. Northumberland's shipbuilding and glass-making industries have also declined. Now the county produces electrical machinery and pottery. The most important industry in Cumbria is power production at the Sellafield nuclear plant. There are manufacturing and engineering industries in parts of Durham and Tyne and Wear. Tyneside was once the country's chief producer of salt, which was extracted from the North Sea.

▲ **The Jarrow Crusade**
In 1936, at the height of the Depression, 200 men marched from Jarrow to London to demand jobs. They were supported along the way by thousands of people.

▲ **Kielder Forest**
Planting of the forest began in 1922. Nearby Kielder Water was created when the Tyne was dammed in the 1970s.

Farming, fishing and forestry

Sheep farming is the main agricultural activity in this bleak and rugged region. Hardy Cheviots are the most common breed. The rivers Eden, Derwent, Tyne and Tweed are all important salmon fisheries. The Kielder Forest, the largest forested area in England, is a major timber producer.

▶ **The Tale of...**
From her home in the Lakes, Beatrix Potter created Squirrel Nutkin, Mrs Tiggywinkle, Jeremy Fisher and other childhood favourites.

◀ **Sellafield**
This power plant on the Irish Sea coast, Cumbria, processes and stores radioactive waste. There is also a visitors' centre, where you can learn about nuclear fuels.

CAN YOU FIND?

1 Durham Cathedral
2 Kielder Water
3 Newcastle-upon-Tyne
4 Sellafield
5 Windermere

see page 47

Cardiff

CARDIFF (CAERDYDD IN WELSH) was made capital of Wales in 1955. It is an ancient settlement on the Bristol Channel at the mouth of the river Taff. The rivers Ely and Rhymney also flow into the estuary. Cardiff's name means 'fort on the Taff,' referring to a Roman fort built there. At one time Cardiff was the world's largest coal-shipping port, handling millions of tonnes of coal each year from the coalfields of South Wales.

▲ Cardiff Castle
Cardiff Castle was designed in the 1800s by William Burges. Its attractions include the Arab Room and the Fairytale Nursery.

The town of Cardiff was slow to grow, and in 1801 it had a population of only 1,870. In the early part of the 19th century the real expansion of Cardiff began. As the Industrial Revolution took hold, coal from across Wales was needed in ever-greater quantities. The docks in Cardiff were linked by canal to the centre of the coal-producing area, as well as to inland ironworks. Although Cardiff's role as a coal-shipping port is now over, the city is still a major seaport with modern docks in the area known as Tiger Bay, recently renamed Cardiff Bay. Cardiff became a city in 1905. Today it covers an area of 140 square kilometres and has a population of 309,400.

Moments in history

According to legend, the Arthurian knight Sir Lancelot sailed from Cardiff after being exiled by King Arthur. The Norman king, William the Conqueror offered his barons the prize of land in Wales if they could subdue the local population. The Normans built Cardiff Castle in the 1100s, and the keep they constructed survives to this day. In the 1700s and 1800s extensive alterations were made to convert the castle into a residence.

◄ Cardiff streets
Most of Cardiff's buildings are modern. There have been many new developments in recent years. The heart of the city is the river Taff, which flows through Bute Park, Cardiff's largest open space.

▲ **Millennium Stadium**
This 75,000-seater stadium is part of the extensive regeneration around the old Tiger Bay. It was built to host the 1999 Rugby World Cup.

▲ **Llandaff Cathedral**
Cardiff's cathedral, in the northern suburb of Llandaff, has been rebuilt many times, but parts of it date from the 1100s.

◀ **City Hall**
Cardiff's City Hall was built in Portland stone during the early 1900s. It is part of the Civic Centre in Cathays Park, which also comprises the Law Courts.

Important buildings

Most of the fine buildings in Cardiff have been built during the past 100 years or so. The Civic Centre in Cathays Park contains the City Hall, the handsome buildings of the Law Courts and the registry (headquarters) of the University of Wales. Llandaff Cathedral, a little way from the city centre, was founded by St Teilo in the AD500s. It is one of the oldest Christian sites in Wales. The present building dates from the 12th and 13th centuries. It was largely destroyed by enemy bombing during World War II, but has been restored. Other buildings of interest include the World Trade Centre, the Welsh National Ice Rink and the Millennium Stadium.

◀ **Cardiff choristers**
Male voice choirs are found in almost every Welsh town or village, but there are more in the south, around the traditional mining areas. Most choirs are run by the Church.

PLACES OF INTEREST

ART GALLERIES
National Gallery

PARKS
Bute Park, Cathays Park, Pontcanna Fields, Sophia Gardens

PLACES OF WORSHIP
Llandaff Cathedral, St John's Church

MUSEUMS
National Museum of Wales, Welsh Industrial & Maritime Museum

OTHER ATTRACTIONS
Cardiff Bay Visitors' Centre, Cardiff Castle, Techniquest

North Wales

MUCH OF NORTH WALES IS COVERED with rugged mountains, dotted with lakes and river valleys. Some spectacular scenery can be found in the region's Snowdonia National Park, which includes the highest peak in the whole of England and Wales, Mount Snowdon.

North Wales consists of five counties. One of them, the island of Anglesey, is separated from the mainland by the Menai Strait. The island's golden beaches are popular with holidaymakers, while the towering cliffs and rock stacks along its coastline attract seabirds. There are lowlands over most of inland Anglesey, in the Lleyn Peninsula and in the river valleys. In the mountainous western part of North Wales is the Snowdonia National Park, which includes several high peaks, including Mount Snowdon. Snowdonia has many lakes. Lake Bala is the largest and is the main source of the river Dee, which flows through North Wales into Cheshire in England, and then to the Irish Sea. Other important rivers include the Clwyd and the Conwy. Several lakes are used as reservoirs, providing water for English cities such as Liverpool and Birmingham.

▼ Donkey derby
The resort of Llandudno on the north coast has been popular with holidaymakers since Victorian times.

Important towns

North Wales has no large cities. The chief town of Anglesey is Llangefni, but the region's best-known place is the village of Llanfairpwllgwyngyll – one version of the village's name runs to 58 letters! In Gwynedd the most important towns are the historic castle towns of Caernarfon and Conwy, and the cathedral and university town of Bangor on the Menai Strait. Llandudno, Colwyn Bay, Rhyl and Prestatyn are popular seaside resorts. Flint is a seaport on the Dee estuary, and Wrexham and Mold are both market towns.

▼ Holyhead
From the port of Holyhead on Holy Island, Anglesey, there are regular ferry and cargo services to Ireland.

▶ Green fields, Gwynedd

COUNTY FACTS

ANGLESEY (YNS MÔN)
Area: 714 sq km
Population: 67,200
Administrative centre:
Llangefni
Other key places: Amlwch,
Beaumaris, Holyhead

CONWY
Area: 1,130 sq km
Population: 111,200
Administrative centre:
Conwy Town
Other key places: Abergele,
Colwyn Bay, Dolgarrog,
Llandudno

DENBIGHSHIRE (SIR DDINBYCH)
Area: 844 sq km
Population: 91,600
Administrative centre: Ruthin
Other key places: Denbigh,
Llangollen, Prestatyn, Rhyl

FLINTSHIRE (SIR Y FFLINT)
Area: 438 sq km
Population: 145,700
Administrative centre: Mold
Other key places: Flint,
Holywell, Queensferry

GWYNEDD
Area: 2,548 sq km
Population: 118,000
Administrative centre:
Caernarfon
Other key places: Bangor,
Bethesda, Ffestiniog,
Porthmadog

WREXHAM (WRECSAM)
Area: 498 sq km
Population: 123,400
Administrative centre:
Wrexham Town
Other key places: Hanmer

Saintly hound

Gelert was Llewellyn of Wales' dog. One day Llewellyn came home to find his baby son's crib empty and Gelert covered in blood. Only after he had killed Gelert did he find his son alive – alongside a dead wolf. Full of remorse, Prince Llewellyn named the dog's burial place in Snowdonia Beddgelert, meaning 'Grave of Gelert.'

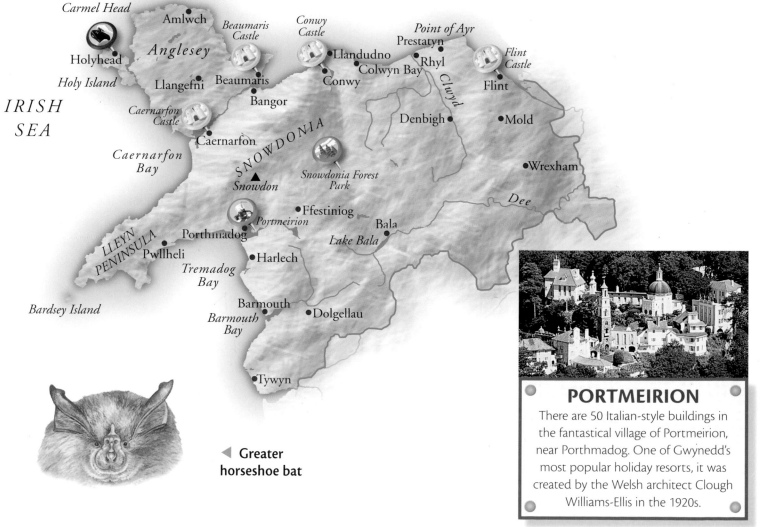

◀ **Greater horseshoe bat**

PORTMEIRION

There are 50 Italian-style buildings in the fantastical village of Portmeirion, near Porthmadog. One of Gwynedd's most popular holiday resorts, it was created by the Welsh architect Clough Williams-Ellis in the 1920s.

▼ Caernarfon Castle

▲ Prehistoric tomb, Bryn Celli

ON THE ISLAND OF ANGLESEY there are remains of settlements built by the Celts who moved into North Wales around 4000BC. At Bryncelli-Dhu, southwest of Menai Bridge, there are ruins of a stone circle, within which is a large stone tomb of a much later date.

When the Romans conquered Britain, two tribes dominated North Wales: the Ordovices and the Deceangli. The region soon came under the control of the Roman garrison at *Deva* (Chester). When the Romans left, more Celtic tribes came into the region from Ireland and from Scotland. The Welsh fiercely opposed the Anglo Saxons who invaded Britain. The resistance was led by a legendary figure called Arthur – not the Round Table hero of the Middle Ages, but a local leader of great military skill.

▼ Flint Castle

CASTLES

After the defeat of Llewellyn, King Edward I built fortresses to protect his strongholds of English settlers:

BEAUMARIS (1295)
Built by James of St George, this is the largest of Edward I's Welsh castles.

CAERNARFON (1283)
Edward's son, the Prince of Wales (later Edward II), was born here in 1284.

CONWY (1282)
Mostly in ruins, this castle has eight impressive towers.

HARLECH (1283)
This was defeated so often it was nicknamed the 'Castle of Lost Causes.'

Glorious Gwynedd

By the AD600s the kingdom, or principality, of Gwynedd dominated North Wales. Rhodri the Great, who ruled from 844 to 877, brought most of Wales under his control. He fought off Viking invasions, but was killed in battle against the English. In 1063 Harold (later King Harold II) and his brother Tostig invaded North Wales and subdued Gwynedd.

Welsh resistance

The Normans kept much of Wales under control, then Gwynedd again led a revival of Welsh self-rule, which lasted from about 1135 to 1282. The last great Welsh leader was Llewellyn the Great, who took the title of Prince of Wales in 1258. He was killed in battle by Edward I of England. Edward built castles to control the Welsh, made his son Prince of Wales in 1301, and split Wales into counties. A final rebellion against England, led by Owen Glendower, was crushed by Henry, Prince of Wales (later Henry V), in 1410.

CAN YOU FIND?

1 Conwy Castle
2 Holyhead
3 Lake Bala
4 Portmeirion
5 Snowdon

see page 53

▲ Conwy Castle
Conwy was built for Edward I in five years flat. The river Conwy's estuary provides a natural moat and so the castle's ruins are reached by bridge.

◄ **Llechwedd Slate Caverns**
From the 1860s, slate from this mine at Blaenau Ffestiniog, Gwynedd, was transported by steam train along the Ffestiniog Railway to Porthmadog.

EISTEDDFODS
An eisteddfod is a Welsh festival of music, poetry and the arts. All the spoken items are in Welsh. Eisteddfods began around 1,000 years ago, as contests between ancient poets called bards. Today there are two main eisteddfods. The Royal National Eisteddfod, which started in the 1850s, is held alternately in North and South Wales. The six-day International Musical Eisteddfod began in 1946 and is held in Llangollen each July. Smaller, local eisteddfods are held in schools and community halls.

Industry

In the 1700s the copper mine on Anglesey was the largest in the world. Quarrying for slate was an important activity in North Wales in the 1800s. Both these industries have now declined. Coalmining and steel production, which were once important industries in the east of the region, have also declined, but there is still an aluminium-smelting plant in the Conwy Valley.

Farming and forestry

Agriculture is the most important activity in North Wales. Beef and dairy cattle are reared in lowland areas, especially on Anglesey, while the hillier parts of North Wales are ideal for sheep farming. There are also large areas of forest in Gwynedd.

▲ **Rupert, Rupert the Bear**
For over 40 years Alfred Bestall produced Rupert comic strips for the *Daily Express*. Bestall lived at Beddgelert. The rugged Snowdonian scenery inspired Nutwood Village, home to tartan-trousered Rupert.

▼ **Portmeirion's prisoner**
Candy-coloured architecture provided the setting for the cult 1960s television series, *The Prisoner*, celebrated here by its fans.

▲ **Herding the sheep**
Plentiful rains feed the lush, green valleys, which in turn feed the farmers' flocks of sheep.

Mid Wales

▼ Brown trout
The river Wye has good stocks of salmon. Fishing is also popular on the Usk, which has wild salmon and brown trout.

▼ Black Mountains
These rounded hills in the southeast of the region extend into the English county of Hereford and Worcester.

MID WALES IS THE LARGEST of the three regions that make up Wales, but it has the smallest population. In the county of Powys there is an average of 24 people per square kilometre, compared with more than 700 in parts of South Wales.

Mid Wales consists of two counties: Powys and Ceredigion. Powys is the largest Welsh county and covers an area equal to a quarter of the whole of Wales. In the east are the Cambrian Mountains, and the Berwyn Mountains run along the northern border of Powys. In the south are the Black Mountains and the Brecon Beacons. The mountain slopes are mostly grassy moorlands, where sheep and cattle graze. The land along the border with England is mostly lowland. Some of the rivers flowing down the mountain valleys produce spectacular waterfalls. The two biggest Welsh rivers, the Severn and the Wye, have their source close together in the west of Mid Wales. Three smaller rivers, the Lyfnant, Rheidol and Ystwyth, rise in the same area. The Wye flows only inside Wales, but the Severn flows into England.

▼ Gushing waters
Features of the Brecon Beacons include fast-flowing streams and sparkling waterfalls.

Important towns
Powys has no large towns, the biggest being Newtown on the river Severn. On the west coast is the important seaside resort and university town of Aberystwyth. Smaller resorts include Aberaeron and New Quay. In the south is the historic county town of Cardigan, at the mouth of the river Teifi. Many of the region's roads are steep and winding because of the mountainous landscape. There are few railways or bus services, and most people travel around by car.

▲ Shy hunter
The weasel-like polecat lives in the woods around the river Vyrnwy. Polecats hunt at night, catching small mammals and birds.

▼ Beautiful views
The Brecon Beacons was made a national park in 1957. Its calm, scenic landscape is perfect for hiking or pony-trekking.

Wildlife

The Vyrnwy nature reserve consists of a lake, woods, moors and meadows. It boasts a wide variety of bird-life, from kingfishers and sandpipers by the lake itself, to sparrowhawks on the moors. There are many species of butterfly in the reserve, too.

▲ **Kingfisher**

COUNTY FACTS

CEREDIGION (SIR CEREDIGION)
Area: 1,795 sq km
Population: 70,200
Administrative centre:
Aberaeron
Other key places:
Aberystwyth, Cardigan,
New Quay

POWYS
Area: 5,196 sq km
Population: 122,300
Administrative centre:
Llandrindod Wells
Other key places: Brecon,
Hay-on-Wye, Newtown,
Welshpool

▲ **Lobster pots**
Fishermen leave baited traps called lobster pots out in Cardigan Bay, marking their positions with floating buoys. Later they haul up the pots for a catch of tasty lobsters.

▼ **Vintage railway**
Aberystwyth's Cliff Railway is the longest electric cliff railway in Britain.

BERWYN MOUNTAINS
Vyrnwy
Powis Castle
Welshpool
Dovey
Machynlleth
Llyfnant
Severn
Newtown
Aberystwyth Castle
Rheidol
Aberystwyth
Ystwyth
Cardigan Bay
Knighton
Rhayader
Llandrindod Wells
CAMBRIAN MOUNTAINS
Offa's Dyke
New Quay
Lampeter
Builth Wells
Llanwrtyd Wells
Hay-on-Wye
Cardigan
Teifi
Wye
Brecon Cathedral
BLACK MOUNTAINS
Brecon
Usk
BRECON BEACONS

G
F
E
D
C
B
A

WATER TRAFFIC

The Brecon and Abergavenny Canal, built in the 19th century, is one of the most picturesque in the British Isles. Over 50 kilometres of the canal are still open to water traffic.

THE EARLIEST KNOWN SETTLERS in Mid Wales were Bronze Age people. You can still find several of their hill forts, stone circles and standing stones. The hill forts in the west were probably connected with Iron Age mines. The Romans occupied little of Mid Wales, but they built strongholds around the Severn and Wye valleys to keep the Britons under control.

The Anglo Saxons thought of Wales as enemy territory, too. To keep the Welsh out of England, the Saxon king Offa of Mercia built a long bank and ditch, known as Offa's Dyke. Some of the best preserved stretches of Offa's Dyke can be seen near the town of Knighton. There, the dyke's bank is around nine metres high, and parts of the ditch are over four metres deep. Part of it runs through Powys. In the west, there were repeated raids by the Irish, and by the Vikings who had occupied Dublin. Irish missionaries, including St David, converted the Welsh to Christianity.

The Middle Ages

The Teifi Valley was ruled for a time by a prince named Ceredig, from which the name Ceredigion comes. The Normans had a difficult time keeping Mid Wales under control. During Llewellyn the Great's rebellion in the 1200s, castles were built at Dolforwyn, near Newtown, and at Montgomery.

▲ **Patron saint**
David, an Irish missionary to Wales, was based for a time at Llandewi Brefi, near Lampeter. A Celtic Cross there is known as St David's Staff.

▼ **Powys Castle**
This medieval castle has changed over the centuries. It includes an Elizabethan gallery and terraced gardens dating from the 1700s.

NATIONAL HERO

Owen Glendower, known to the Welsh as Owain Glyn Dwr, was the last of the great Welsh princes. He was born in in the 1350s. As the heir of the princes of Powys, he owned large estates. Following a quarrel with an English neighbour he started a rebellion against English rule in 1400. After early successes he set up an independent Welsh parliament. But in 1405 Henry, Prince of Wales (later King Henry V), began a series of campaigns against him. By 1409 Glendower was a fugitive. After a last campaign in 1410 he disappeared. He is thought to have died around 1416.

Troubled times

Owen Glendower's rebellion in the 1400s led to fighting in the region. He is said to have held a parliament at Machynlleth, and kept court at Aberystwyth. Welsh castles were held for Charles I during the English Civil War in the 1600s. Charles set up a mint at Aberystwyth before the war, and used silver from local mines to equip his armies. Parliamentary forces besieged and captured the castle, and then blew it up. They also destroyed Cardigan Castle.

Centre for Alternative Technology

Founded in 1975, CAT was built on an old slate mine near Machynlleth, Powys. Today, it is the most important environmental centre in Europe. There are over 50 exhibits, including eco-friendly homes, organic gardens and a water-powered cliff railway. Even the telephone boxes are solar-powered!

◀ **The race is on!**
The spa town of Llanwrtyd Wells hosts the Man vs Horse Marathon. A person who outruns a horse on the course could win £10,000 – but no one has managed to claim the prize yet!

Industry and farming

Most manufacturing industry has been introduced into the region since about 1950. There is some quarrying, mostly of limestone and granite. Lead mining, which was once a flourishing industry, has mostly disappeared. Cattle and sheep rearing are the main farming activities. The biggest source of income in the region, however, is tourism. Walkers, cavers and hang-gliders are attracted to the Brecon Beacons National Park.

Festivals

Two summer festivals attract extra tourists to Mid Wales each year. The market town of Hay-on-Wye is the second-hand book capital of Britain. Its Festival of Literature brings many visitors, as well as leading authors and poets who gather there to give readings of their works. In addition, thousands of jazz enthusiasts from all over Europe gather at Brecon each August for the Brecon Jazz Festival.

▲ **World Bog Snorkelling Championships**
Each August, bog snorkellers assemble in Llanwrtyd Wells. Competitors must swim two lengths of the 55-metre-long peat bog trench and are only allowed to surface twice.

▲ **Welsh lovespoon**
Brecknock Museum has a large collection of traditional lovespoons. From the 1600s, men gave these wooden spoons to their lovers. They carved symbols into the spoons: a cross, for example, symbolized faith.

CAN YOU FIND?

1 Aberystwyth
2 Brecon Beacons
3 Hay-on-Wye
4 Llanwrtyd Wells
5 Powis Castle

see page 57

▲ **Second-hand books, Hay-on-Wye**

South Wales

▼ **Tenby harbour**
Georgian houses overlook the pretty harbour at Tenby, Pembrokeshire.

SOUTH WALES IS THE MOST INDUSTRIALIZED and thickly-populated region of Wales. For over 200 years the huge coalfield beneath the east of the region provided work for hundreds of thousands of miners, but most of the coal-mines have now closed down.

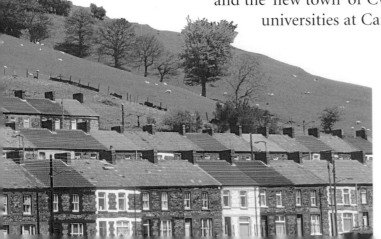

The landscape of South Wales consists mostly of river valleys leading down from the Brecon Beacons, and low-lying coastal areas. The Prescelli Mountains are a feature of Pembrokeshire. The Gower Peninsula, near Swansea, is long and narrow, with a rocky coastline and wide, sandy beaches. It is a popular area for holidaymakers. Milford Haven and Swansea Bay both form large, natural harbours, making them ideal locations for ports. Huge supertankers from all over the world unload their cargo at the oil port at Milford Haven.

▼ **St David's Head**
This headland is north-west of St David's and is part of the National Park. Wild flowers, such as pink thrift, bloom along the coastal paths.

Important towns

The largest cities and towns in Wales lie in the south. Cardiff, the capital, is a seaport and centre of business and government. At one time it was the largest coal-shipping port in the world. Swansea, the region's second-largest city, is another major seaport. Other important towns include Haverfordwest, Carmarthen, Port Talbot, Bridgend, Newport and the 'new town' of Cwmbran. There are universities at Cardiff and Swansea.

▼ **Rhondda Valley**
Rows of identical terraced houses were built in South Wales for the workers of the coal seams.

▶ **Marking the millennium**
The showpiece of Cardiff's new architecture is the Stadiwm y Mileniwm, or Millennium Stadium, which opened in 1999.

COUNTY FACTS

BLAENAU GWENT
Area: 140 sq km
Population: 73,200
Administrative centre:
Ebbw Vale
Other key places:
Abertillery, Tredegar

BRIDGEND
(PEN-Y-BONT AR OGWR)
Area: 246 sq km
Population: 130,700
Administrative centre:
Bridgend
Other key places:
Maesteg, Porthcawl

CAERPHILLY (CAERFFILI)
Area: 278 sq km
Population: 170,000
Administrative centre:
Hengoed
Other key places:
Abercarn, Caerphilly

CARDIFF (CAERDYDD)
Area: 140 sq km
Population: 309,400
Administrative centre:
Cardiff City

CARMARTHENSHIRE
(SIR CAERFYRDDIN)
Area: 2,395 sq km
Population: 169,000
Administrative centre:
Carmarthen
Other key places:
Laugharne, Llanelli

MERTHYR TYDFIL
(MERTHYR TUDFUL)
Area: 111 sq km
Population: 58,700
Administrative centre:
Merthyr Tydfil

MONMOUTHSHIRE
(SIR FYNWY)
Area: 850 sq km
Population: 85,600
Administrative centre:
Cwmbran
Other key places:
Abergavenny, Caldicot,
Chepstow, Monmouth

NEATH PORT TALBOT
(CASTELL-NEDD
PORT TALBOT)
Area: 442 sq km
Population: 139,600
Administrative centre:
Port Talbot
Other key places: Neath

NEWPORT
(CAESNEWYDD-
AR-WYSG)
Area: 190 sq km
Population: 137,200
Administrative centre:
Newport

PEMBROKESHIRE
(SIR BENFRO)
Area: 1,590 sq km
Population: 114,000
Administrative centre:
Haverfordwest
Other key places:
Fishguard, Milford Haven,
Pembroke, Tenby

RHONDDA, CYNON, TAFF
(RHONDDA, CYNON, TAF)
Area: 424 sq km
Population: 240,000
Administrative centre:
Tonypandy
Other key places:
Llantrisant, Pontypridd

SWANSEA (ABERTAWE)
Area: 378 sq km
Population: 230,600
Administrative centre:
Swansea City

Eco-tragedy

In February 1996 Pembrokeshire hit the headlines when the oil supertanker *Sea Empress* ran aground in Milford Sound. The tanker spilt over 75,000 tonnes of crude oil into the sea. More than 190 kilometres of coastline were coated in oil. The ecological disaster wiped out a colony of rare starfish in West Angle Bay.

SURF'S UP!

The wild west coast of Pembrokeshire is a hit with surfers – of both the human and animal kind! Top destinations include the villages of Dale, Newgale and St David's.

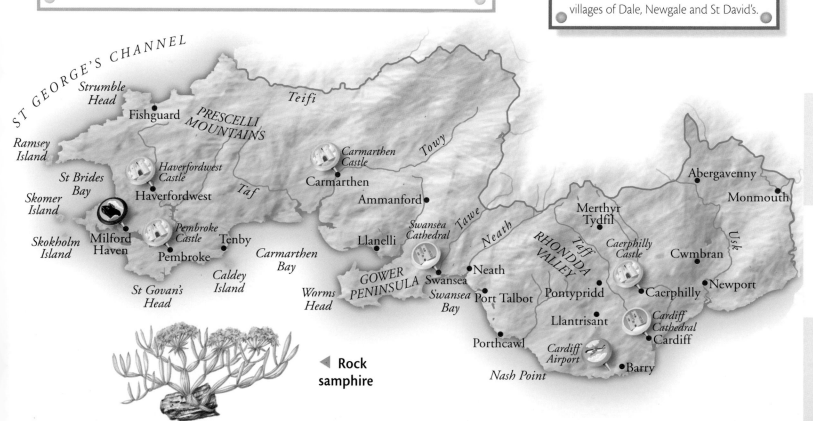

◄ Rock samphire

▲ **Place of rest**
The stone frame of a cromlech, or tomb, can still be seen at Pentre Ifanin, Pembrokeshire.

THE SILURES, AN ANCIENT BRITISH tribe, were living in South Wales when the Romans invaded Britain. The Romans built roads and forts in the region and at Caerwent you can see the remains of *Venta Silurum*, a Roman settlement.

By the time of the Norman conquest there were two strong states in South Wales: Deheubarth in the southwest, and Glamorgan and Gwent in the southeast. But few Welsh states remained strong for long, because of the Welsh rules of inheritance, known as gavelkind. When a man died, his estates were divided equally among his sons. So each time a power base was built up by a ruler, it was split up again on his death.

WHAT'S IN A NAME?
The Welsh name for the seaport of Tenby is Dinbych y Pysgod. The literal translation is the 'Little Fort of the Fishes.'

Norman control

Rhys ap Tewdwr became king of South Wales in 1078, but was killed in battle against the Normans. His grandson, Rhys ap Gruffydd, had a long struggle with Henry II, but eventually acknowledged the English king as his overlord and took the title of Lord Rhys. By the 1200s most of South Wales was controlled by the Normans and the region's Celtic Church was brought under the authority of the Archbishop of Canterbury.

◄ **Caerleon**
Roman ruins at Caerleon, known then as *Isca*, include baths, an amphitheatre and barracks.

CAN YOU FIND?
1 Caerphilly Castle
2 Cardiff
3 Gower Peninsula
4 Milford Haven
5 Swansea Cathedral

see page 61

◄ **Manorbier Castle**
In some of the rooms of this 12th-century coastal castle are waxwork cast-offs from Madame Tussaud's in London. The figures include two rejected 'Prince Philips'!

◄ Roald Dahl
The Cardiff suburb of Llandaff was home to Norwegian immigrants, and the birthplace of author Roald Dahl. In *Boy*, Dahl described his years at Llandaff Cathedral School.

▲ Sport of Wales
In addition to the big-name clubs, there are countless smaller rugby teams with plenty of local support.

◄ Oil refinery
At night, Milford Haven looks like something out of a fairytale. Its refineries are lit up with twinkling lights.

WELSH RUGBY

CARDIFF SARACENS RFC (1966)
Cardiff is home to 47 different clubs, including the 'Sarries,' or Saracens. The club was born when Roath Park (1889) and the Spillers (1920) joined forces.

SWANSEA RFC (1872)
Swansea players wear a white strip and are known as the Great Whites.

NEATH RFC (1871)
Neath's players are nicknamed the Welsh All Blacks. Their black jerseys are decorated with a white Maltese cross.

LLANELLI RFC (1876)
The highpoint of Llanelli's history was its defeat of the New Zealand All Blacks in 1972. Since 1885, players have worn the famous red jersey, hence the nickname the 'Scarlets'.

Castles

A chain of more than twenty castles lies along the coast of South Wales. Most were built by Norman lords to claim their ownership of the land. The most important, which is built slightly inland, is Caerphilly. The largest castle in Wales, it is surrounded by a moat and two lakes. The ruins of Chepstow Castle are long and narrow, because they stand on the bank of the river Wye. Cardiff Castle is well preserved, and part of it now houses a music school. The remains of Kenfig Castle were buried in sand by a storm in the 1500s.

▼ Tintern Abbey
Tintern Abbey, on the banks of the river Wye, was destroyed on the orders of Henry VIII. In the 1790s, its ruins inspired the poet Wordsworth and painter Turner.

Industry

During the 1800s Welsh industry was based on coalmining and steel production, with Swansea the copper-smelting capital of the world. Valleys such as the Rhondda were lined with pits, producing coal for export and for use in the Welsh steelworks. Demand for coal fell off after World War I (1914–18) and has continued to drop. There are still large steelworks, but factories in the region also make electronic components, car parts and plastics. There is a major oil refinery beside the deep-water tanker terminal at Milford Haven.

Farming

Cattle rearing and sheep farming are the main agricultural activities. Many small towns, such as Carmarthen, hold regular markets where livestock is bought and sold. These are also the places to buy local specialities such as cockles and laver bread (cooked seaweed).

▲ Harvesting seaweed for laver bread

Channel Islands

▼ **Wind and sails**
Yachts dot the seas around the islands. There are marinas at St Helier, Jersey, and St Peter Port, Guernsey.

THE CHANNEL ISLANDS LIE NEAR THE WEST COAST of France, not far from the Cherbourg Peninsula. They are not part of the United Kingdom, but are dependencies of the British Crown. The British Government is responsible for their international relations and defence.

▲ **Jersey cow**
Jersey and Guernsey both have their own native breeds of dairy cattle. Jersey milk is very rich and creamy.

Jersey is the largest island, then Guernsey. Seven smaller islands form part of Guernsey: Alderney, Brechou, Herm, Jethou, Lihou, Great Sark and Little Sark. The Channel Islands also include Burhou, a tiny islet, and the barren rocks and reefs off the main islands. The islands are a mix of steep cliffs, sandy beaches and wide plains. Their mild climate is ideal for growing flowers and vegetables for export, and also attracts many holidaymakers each year.

Language and law

Channel Islanders speak English and French, and some speak a dialect of old Norman French. Jersey, Guernsey and Alderney have their own law-making assemblies called States, and Sark has one called the Court of Chief Pleas. All the islands issue their own currency and stamps. Most have low income tax rates, and Sark has none at all.

▼ **Fields of flowers**
Flowers grown on the islands, such as freesias and tulips, are exported daily to mainland Britain.

History of the islands

The Channel Islands were part of the Duchy of Normandy when William the Conqueror invaded England in 1066. Ever since, they have been attached to the English monarchy. Apart from raids by the Scots and the French, the Channel Islands have only been invaded once – by the Germans, who occupied them from July 1940 to May 1945. There are many remains of the fortifications they built. Earlier forts include Jersey's Mount Orgueil Castle, which was built in the Middle Ages.

ENGLISH CHANNEL
St Anne • Alderney

Herm
Guernsey St Peter Port Great Sark
Little Sark

Jersey Airport
Jersey St Helier

ISLAND FACTS

Jersey
Area: 11,630 hectares
Population: 84,082
Capital: St Helier

Guernsey
Area: 6,340 hectares
Population: 58,867
Capital: St Peter Port

Alderney
Area: 795 hectares
Population: 2,297
Chief town: St Anne

Brechou
Area: 30 hectares

Great Sark
Area: 419 hectares

Herm
Area: 130 hectares

Jethou
Area: 18 hectares

Lihou
Area: 15 hectares

Little Sark
Area: 97 hectares

Isle of Man

▼**Peel Castle**
This 11th-century castle sits on St Patrick's Island. It is joined to the tiny town of Peel by a causeway.

THE ISLE OF MAN IS IN THE IRISH SEA. It lies about the same distance from each of England, Scotland, Wales and Ireland. The Isle of Man is a Crown dependency: it has its own legal system, but some British laws apply there, too. The Queen, known as the Lord of Man, is represented on the island by a lieutenant governor.

The island has a large lowland area in the north, known as the Ayres, below which stretches a mountain range. At 621 metres, Snaefell is the highest point. The west and east coasts are rugged, with many cliffs and bays. To the south is an islet, the Calf of Man, which is a bird sanctuary.

▼ **The Tynwald**
The Isle of Man has the world's oldest continuous parliament, the Tynwald. It was founded in AD979. Every July 5th, the parliamentary ceremony is held at St John's.

Island life

The first Manxpeople were Celts. For centuries they spoke a form of Gaelic, but few speak it today. Vikings settled the island from the AD800s. The Isle of Man was successively ruled by Norway, Scotland and England. Then Henry IV granted the island to the Stanley family, who governed it for more than 300 years. It was bought back by the British Crown in the 1700s.

ISLAND FACTS

Isle of Man
Area: 572 sq km
Population: 69,788
Capital: Douglas
Other key places: Castletown, Peel, Ramsey

Industry, tourism and farming

In the past, smuggling and lead mining were important sources of revenue. Today the island's low rate of income tax attracts people to invest in Manx banks. Tourism is also big business. The island's farmers grow cereal and root crops, and raise cattle and sheep.

D

C

Point of Ayre

Ramsey Bay

Sulby
Ramsey *Maughgold Head*

Peel Castle
Neb *Snaefell*
Peel

B

Dhoo
Castle Rushen *Douglas*

Bradda Head

Calf of Man *Castletown*

◄ **Tourist Trophy**
Motorcyclists flock to the Isle of Man each summer to take part in the island's Tourist Trophy.

IRISH SEA

A

Scotland

SCOTLAND IS THE NORTHERNMOST PART of the island of Great Britain, making up about one-third of its total area. In addition to the mainland, Scotland has hundreds of offshore islands, which can be divided in three major groups: the Hebrides off the west coast, and the Orkney Islands and Shetland Islands to the north. Edinburgh is Scotland's capital city.

◀ Scottish thistle
In the 1400s James III of Scotland made the thistle his royal emblem. There is still an order of Scottish knights known as the Knights of the Thistle.

The earliest settlers arrived in Scotland about 8,000 years ago. When the Romans arrived in AD70, the inhabitants of Scotland living north of the river Clyde were mostly Picts, while British tribes lived in the border area. Later invaders were the Scots from Ireland, the Angles from Germany and the Vikings from Scandinavia.

▲ The Scottish Highlands
One of Scotland's chief landmarks is Ben Nevis, Britain's highest mountain. It rises to a height of 1,343 metres.

Kenneth MacAlpin, a Scottish king, ruled the country in the AD800s. The first person to rule the whole country was Malcolm II, who came to the throne in 1005. Throughout the Middle Ages there were wars between Scotland and England. Edward I of England tried to conquer Scotland in the 1300s, but eventually Robert the Bruce secured Scotland's independence in 1328. The Stewarts, who were descended from Robert the Bruce's daughter Marjorie, ruled Scotland for the next 300 years.

Scotland became linked to England when the Stuart king, James VI of Scotland, succeeded the English queen, Elizabeth I, in 1603. In 1707 an Act of Union formally joined the two countries.

▲ River Tay
Scotland's earliest settlements were built near sources of fresh water.

▼ Iron Age builders
The Picts were warlike people who settled northeastern Scotland. They lived in underground houses, known as weems, and built defensive round towers, known as brochs.

◀ Patron saint of Scotland
Andrew is Russia's patron saint as well as Scotland's. He was one of Christ's disciples. Like Christ, Andrew was crucified, which is why his symbol is a cross.

Government of Scotland

Today Scotland is part of the United Kingdom of Great Britain and Northern Ireland. However, Scotland has its own legal, educational and local government systems. In 1999 the Scottish Parliament took control of many of Scotland's affairs for the first time in almost 300 years.

The Scottish Parliament

The Parliament, which consists of 129 MPs elected by the Scottish people, meets in Edinburgh. An executive consisting of a First Minister and other ministers is in charge. The Secretary of State for Scotland remains in the Cabinet of the UK government, and liaises with the First Minister. Foreign, defence, and economic matters are the responsibility of the Parliament at Westminster.

▲ **Robert I of Scotland**
Robert the Bruce was crowned king of Scotland in 1306. Almost at once he was on the run from the armies of Edward I, and later Edward II, of England. Robert finally defeated the English at Bannockburn in 1314.

COUNTRY FACTS

SCOTLAND
Area: 78,789 sq km
Population: 5,128,000
Capital: Edinburgh
Major cities: Aberdeen, Dundee, Glasgow
Official language: English (Scottish Gaelic is spoken by 1.4 percent of the population)
Main religions: Church of Scotland (Presbyterian), Scottish Episcopal Church, Roman Catholicism
Currency: Pound sterling (£)
Highest point: Ben Nevis (1,343 m)
Longest river: Tay (188 km)
Largest lake: Loch Lomond (60 sq km)

▼ **James VI's family tree**
The Scottish king, James VI, traced his ancestry back more than two centuries to heroic Robert the Bruce.

▼ **Church of Scotland**
The Calvinist John Knox founded the Presbyterian Church of Scotland in the 1500s. This was a break away from the Roman Catholic Church. There is a statue of Knox in front of St Giles' Cathedral, Edinburgh, where he was dean.

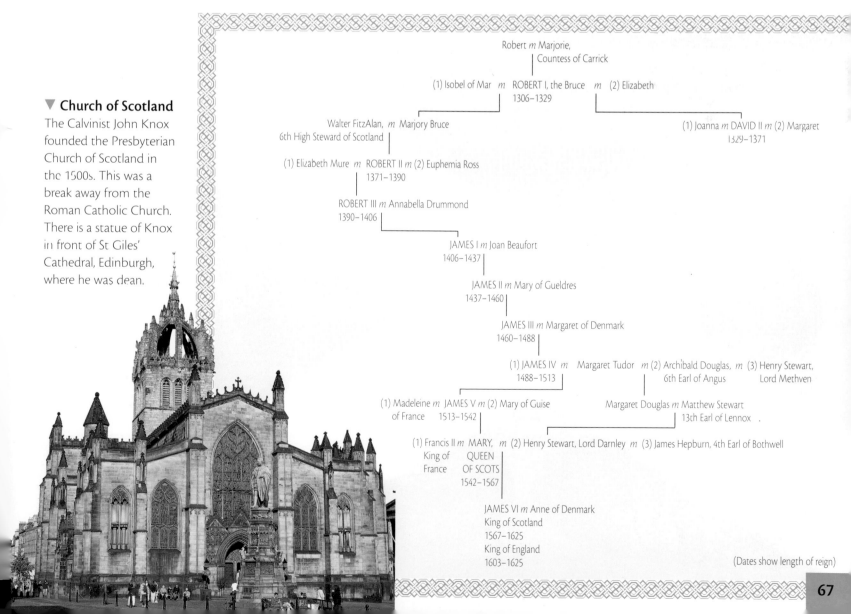

Robert *m* Marjorie, Countess of Carrick

(1) Isobel of Mar *m* ROBERT I, the Bruce *m* (2) Elizabeth
1306–1329

Walter FitzAlan, *m* Marjory Bruce
6th High Steward of Scotland

(1) Joanna *m* DAVID II *m* (2) Margaret
1329–1371

(1) Elizabeth Mure *m* ROBERT II *m* (2) Euphemia Ross
1371–1390

ROBERT III *m* Annabella Drummond
1390–1406

JAMES I *m* Joan Beaufort
1406–1437

JAMES II *m* Mary of Gueldres
1437–1460

JAMES III *m* Margaret of Denmark
1460–1488

(1) JAMES IV *m* Margaret Tudor *m* (2) Archibald Douglas, *m* (3) Henry Stewart,
1488–1513   6th Earl of Angus   Lord Methven

(1) Madeleine *m* JAMES V *m* (2) Mary of Guise
of France   1513–1542

Margaret Douglas *m* Matthew Stewart
13th Earl of Lennox

(1) Francis II *m* MARY, *m* (2) Henry Stewart, Lord Darnley *m* (3) James Hepburn, 4th Earl of Bothwell
King of   QUEEN
France   OF SCOTS
             1542–1567

JAMES VI *m* Anne of Denmark
King of Scotland
1567–1625
King of England
1603–1625

(Dates show length of reign)

Scotland
Physical features

Snot surprising when you discover that, more than 400 million years ago, the two countries were on different continents. The two land masses collided, and it is possible to trace where they joined together deep under the border area of Scotland and England. Scotland's rugged mountains and scenery are the result of movements in the Earth's crust over millions of years.

Three geographical regions make up mainland Scotland. Bordering England are the Southern Uplands, which consist mostly of rolling moors with fertile soil. In the south, the Cheviot Hills form the border with England. Next come the Central Lowlands, through which three major rivers, the Clyde, the Forth and the Tay, flow. This area has the best farmland and mineral resources. The third region is the Highlands, which cover two-thirds of the country. This region is mountainous, with jagged peaks and numerous lakes, known as lochs. The most mountainous part is in the west. Most people in the Highland region live in the coastal lowlands, especially in the east.

▼ The Scottish 'Alps'
Winter snow on the Highland slopes provides good skiing opportunities at Aviemore.

▲ Mountain landscape
Scotland's mountains were shaped by glaciers, moving sheets of ice that covered the land during the last Ice Age.

▲ Loch Duich
Glaciers carved out hollows in the surface of the land. These have since filled with water to form the hundreds of lochs which are such a feature of the Highlands.

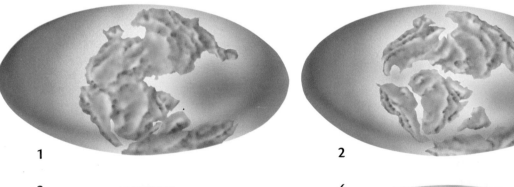

1

2

3

4

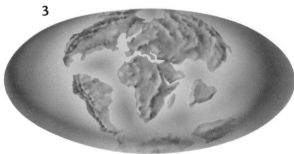

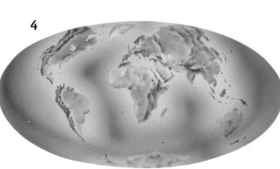

◄ Shifting lands
Once separated by sea, Scotland and England were pushed together as a result of continental drift. This was the movement of the Earth's land masses that took place over a period of millions of years:
1 Around 280 mya, the land formed one giant supercontinent, Pangaea
2 Around 180 mya, Pangaea split into Laurasia (to the north) and Gondwanaland (to the south)
3 Around 65 mya, the Atlantic Ocean widened
4 Today, the land masses are grouped into seven continents

◄ Stormy seas
The rocky Grampian coast takes a regular battering from the North Sea waves.

CLIMATE
Scotland's climate is mainly mild, but it is cooler and wetter than the climate of England and Wales. The prevailing winds come from the southwest. They bring a series of weather fronts across the island. Scotland, like Wales, parts of western England and northern Ireland, receives more rain than eastern England.
Rainfall is lower along Scotland's east coast because of the so-called 'rain shadow' cast by the mountains. The average annual rainfall in Edinburgh is 750–1,000 mm, while in the west of Scotland it is more than 1,500 mm. During the winter months, snow falls in the Highlands.

ATLANTIC OCEAN

NORTH SEA

Moving mountains

When the Atlantic Ocean began to open up about sixty-five million years ago, the land which is now Scotland remained joined to what is now Europe. The rest of that continent formed what is now North America. The hard rocks that make up Scotland's mountains were crushed, folded and distorted many times – and even turned upside down! Originally the mountains were sharp and jagged. Millions of years of action by wind, rain and ice have worn them down, so they are much lower than their original height with rounded outlines.

◄ Highs and lows
The Scottish Lowlands are the best region for arable farming. In the Highlands, farmers raise sheep and a breed of hardy beef cattle, known as the Aberdeen Angus.

▲ Firth of Forth
The river Forth, with its long estuary, or firth, marks the dividing line between the Highlands and the rest of Scotland.

The Great Glen

Glen Mor, or the Great Glen, is the remains of a huge geological fault in the Earth's crust. It may once have been similar to the earthquake-prone San Andreas Fault in California, where two of the Earth's plates are grating against one another.

Edinburgh

EDINBURGH HAS BEEN THE CAPITAL OF SCOTLAND since the beginning of the 15th century, when it replaced the Scottish capital of Perth. In 1999 it became the seat of the revived Scottish Parliament. Built around the banks of the Forth Estuary, Edinburgh is ideally sited in the Central Lowlands, a region of rich farmland and extensive mineral deposits.

Edinburgh has direct rail and road links with London, and air services link it with United Kingdom cities and several capital cities in continental Europe. Rail and road bridges span the Firth of Forth to link the city with the northern part of the country. There are many different industries in and around the capital, including brewing, whisky distilling, and textile and paper manufacturing. Edinburgh is also a key business centre, with many banks and insurance offices.

▲ **Unfinished business**
Funds to build the Greek-style National Monument, atop Calton Hill, ran out after just 12 columns were complete.

▼ **Royal guesthouse**
The Palace of Holyroodhouse is the Queen's official residence in Scotland.

Important buildings

The magnificent castle, perched high up on its rocky crag, dominates the city. It stands on the plug of a long-dead volcano. To the north of the castle rock is a valley through which the railway line runs, and on the far side is Princes Street, one of the main shopping centres. Nearby is Calton Hill, another volcanic plug, which is topped by the Nelson Monument. To the east of the city is the magnificent hill of Arthur's Seat, set in Holyrood Park. On the edge of the park stands the Palace of Holyroodhouse. Several Scottish kings and queens are buried in the palace's vault. Other notable buildings include St Giles' Cathedral, the Royal Observatory on Calton Hill, and Register House.

▲ **Street juggler**
Edinburgh's International Festival of Music and Dance attracts hoards of tourists to the city each August. Performers include actors, comedians and street entertainers.

▼ **Museum of Scotland**
Opened in 1998, the new Museum of Scotland houses a collection of artefacts from Scottish history.

PLACES OF INTEREST

ART GALLERIES
National Gallery of Scotland, Royal Scottish Academy, Scottish National Gallery of Modern Art, Scottish National Portrait Gallery

PARKS
Holyrood Park, Meadow Park, Princes Street Gardens, Ramsay Garden, Royal Terrace Gardens

PLACES OF WORSHIP
Canongate Kirk, Greyfriars Kirk, Highland Tolbooth Kirk, St Giles' Cathedral, St Mary's Episcopal Cathedral, Tron Kirk

MUSEUMS
Museum of Childhood, Museum of Scotland, The People's Story, Royal Museum of Scotland, Scotch Whisky Heritage Centre, The Writers' Museum

OTHER ATTRACTIONS
Abbey Lairds, Arthur's Seat, Camera Obscura, Edinburgh Castle, Edinburgh Experience, Flodden Wall, National Monument, Palace of Holyroodhouse, Royal Botanic Garden

The oldest of the city's three universities was founded in 1583. In addition, Edinburgh boasts two famous medical colleges: the Royal College of Physicians of Edinburgh and the Royal College of Surgeons of Edinburgh. The Meadowbank Sports Centre hosted the 1970 Commonwealth Games.

▲ **Edinburgh streets**
Many of Edinburgh's buildings date to the 1700s. The 37-km-long Water of Leith meanders through the city.

Moments in history

There has been a settlement at Edinburgh since 850BC. Edinburgh grew in the AD1000s when David I established his court at Edinburgh Castle. In 1513 the English defeated the Scots at the Battle of Flodden, killing James IV and 10,000 of his men. Remains of Flodden Wall can still be seen on the High Street. When James VI became king of England in 1603, the royal court moved to London. In the 1700s many new buildings were erected to the north of the old city. In the 1800s the population of the city quadrupled, and many terraced houses were built. Today, the city has a population of 420,170.

◀ **Regimental entertainment**
Against the impressive backdrop of the castle, Edinburgh's Military Tattoo is held at the end of August each year, to coincide with the Edinburgh Festival.

◀ **Wall plaque, the Royal Mile**
Leading up to Edinburgh Castle, the Royal Mile is lined with beautiful buildings, some dating to the 1400s.

▲ **Seat of learning**
Students of Edinburgh University have included Charles Darwin, writers Thomas Carlyle and Sir Walter Scott, and the inventor Alexander Graham Bell.

Dumfries and Galloway

▼ Poem in stone
Ruthwell Cross dates from the AD700s. It is covered with ancient runes, or writing. The inscription includes part of an Old English poem called *The Dream of the Rood*, which is about Christ's crucifixion.

▼ Religious ruins
Sweetheart Abbey, near Kirkcudbright, was a centre for Cistercian monks from 1273 until 1603.

THE DUMFRIES AND GALLOWAY REGION lies in southwestern Scotland. It contains the former counties of Dumfriesshire, Kirkcudbrightshire and Wigtownshire. Ireland is only a few kilometres away across a stretch of water called the North Channel.

Most of this region is low-lying coastal land, broken up by rocky headlands. To the north lies a plateau of moorland. In the west is a hammer-head shaped peninsula called the Rhins of Galloway. It stretches south to the Mull of Galloway, a towering 64-metre-high cliff. In the northern part of the Rhins is the port of Stranraer, which runs a regular shipping service to Larne in Northern Ireland.

◀ Rose-tinted fortress
Caerlaverock Castle has stood on the shores of the Solway Firth since the 1290s. It was built from unusual, pinkish-coloured stone.

Farming and industry
Farmers in Dumfries and Galloway rear sheep, cattle and pigs, and grow oats, turnips and other cattle feed. Potatoes are the main crop grown for human consumption. There are five hydroelectric power stations in Kirkcudbrightshire, which use water from local rivers and lochs to generate electricity. Wigtown is being developed as the centre of Scotland's book trade. Tourism is important in the region. Kirkcudbright attracts artists and anglers. The fishing is also good at Gatehouse of Fleet on the river Fleet.

▲ Barnacle goose

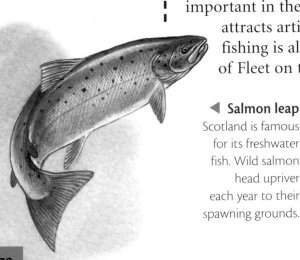

◀ Salmon leap
Scotland is famous for its freshwater fish. Wild salmon head upriver each year to their spawning grounds.

▶ Power station
This hydroelectric dam harnesses water power. The energy of water driving a turbine is changed into electrical energy at the power station.

Moments in history

People have lived in this region since around 5000BC. The Stone Age tombs at Cairnholy, near Gatehouse of Fleet, date from about 3000BC. At Burnswark, near Lockerbie, you can see the remains of an Iron Age hill fort and two Roman camps. St Ninian, who founded a monastery at Whithorn, near Burrow Head, is said to have brought Christianity to the area during the 4th century. Later, Viking invaders from Scandinavia and Normans from England occupied the area. It became a Scottish shire, or county, in the 1400s.

▲ Viking invaders

COUNTY FACTS

DUMFRIES AND GALLOWAY
Area: 6,370 sq km
Population: 144,856
Administrative centre: Dumfries
Other towns: Kirkcudbright, Stranraer

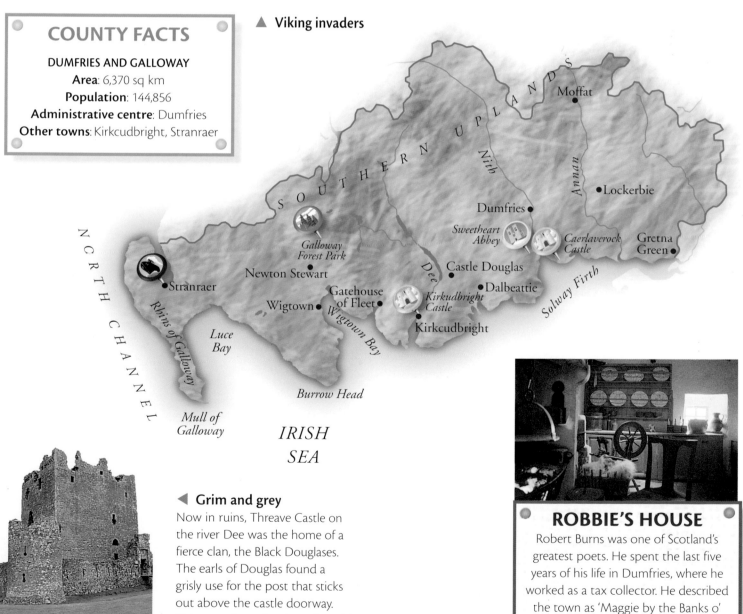

F

E

D

C

B

A

Moffat

SOUTHERN UPLANDS

Nith

Annan

Lockerbie

Dumfries

Sweetheart Abbey

Caerlaverock Castle

Gretna Green

Castle Douglas

Dalbeattie

Solway Firth

Galloway Forest Park

Newton Stewart

Dee

Gatehouse of Fleet

Kirkudbright Castle

NORTH CHANNEL

Rhins of Galloway

Wigtown

Wigtown Bay

Kirkcudbright

Stranraer

Luce Bay

Burrow Head

Mull of Galloway

IRISH SEA

◄ Grim and grey

Now in ruins, Threave Castle on the river Dee was the home of a fierce clan, the Black Douglases. The earls of Douglas found a grisly use for the post that sticks out above the castle doorway. This was where they hung 'tassels' – that is, their poor enemies!

ROBBIE'S HOUSE

Robert Burns was one of Scotland's greatest poets. He spent the last five years of his life in Dumfries, where he worked as a tax collector. He described the town as 'Maggie by the Banks o' Nith.' His house is now a museum.

Borders

▼ **Order of the Garter**
Coldstream, on the banks of the river Tweed, was the birthplace of the British Army's oldest regiment, the Coldstream Guards. The regiment's emblem is the Star of the Order of the Garter.

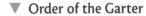

▼ **Melrose Abbey**
These Gothic ruins near Galashiels were restored by Sir Walter Scott in the 1800s. Robert the Bruce's heart is buried here.

THE SCOTTISH BORDERS HAS A LONG FRONTIER with England, sloping from southwest to northeast. Much of the land on either side of the border is wild country, with steep hills, fast-flowing streams and few towns or villages. The Borders region replaced the historic counties of Berwickshire, Peeblesshire, Roxburghshire and Selkirkshire.

Most of the land in the Scottish Borders forms part of the Southern Uplands. These well-worn, rounded hills are covered with grass and heather. They include the Cheviots along the English border – the highest peak is The Cheviot (816 metres). To the north are the Pentland, Moorfoot and Lammermuir Hills. In the east is a lowland area called the Merse, a rich farming region. The river Tweed, with its many tributaries, flows between the hills and through the fertile Merse to the sea. The region has warm summers and cold winters. Its rainfall is very variable, ranging from 625 to 1,750 mm per year.

◀ **Boats of Berwickshire**
Eyemouth is the region's chief fishing harbour.

Farming and industry

About half of the land in the Borders is used for grazing sheep and cattle. Farmers grow barley, wheat and potatoes, and grass, turnips and other crops for animal feed. Ettrick Forest is the remains of a huge ancient forest, and there are modern plantations of pine. Foxes, badgers and rabbits are common, and roe-deer live in some of the forests. Salmon breed in the river Tweed. There is a small amount of industry, largely textiles, with tweed cloth as the main output. Jedburgh is a centre of the tweed industry.

◀ **Scots pine**

▶ **Rabbit**

▶ **River Tweed**

Moments in history

The Borders were part of the English kingdom of Northumbria until the early AD1000s, when the region was taken into Scotland. An exception was the town of Berwick-upon-Tweed, which changed hands between England and Scotland several times before finally becoming part of England in 1482. At the same time, powerful Scottish families, such as the Douglases, competed with one another for power. Greenknowe Tower, near Earlston, was built as a stronghold in 1581, when border skirmishes were still common.

▲ **Greedy reivers**
From the 1200s to the 1500s the whole area of the Borders was ravaged by wars, skirmishes and reiving (plundering).

NORTH SEA

MOORFOOT HILLS
▲ *Blackhope Scar*
Peebles •
Tweed
Abbotsford
Galashiels •
Melrose Abbey
Coldstream •
Kelso
Melrose •
Selkirk •
Roxburgh •
Teviot
Ettrick Forest
• Jedburgh
Ettrick
• Hawick
CHEVIOT HILLS
Eyemouth •
Duns
Tweed

COUNTY FACTS

BORDERS
Area: 4,675 sq km
Population: 105,300
Administrative centre: Melrose
Other cities: Duns, Jedburgh, Peebles, Selkirk

▶ **Duns Scotus**

WHAT'S IN A NAME?
The Franciscan priest and philosopher Duns Scotus was born at Duns in Berwickshire in 1265. The word 'dunce' comes from his name, because his followers were supposed to be against learning.

▲ **Romantic house**
Abbotsford is a large house near Melrose. It was built by the novelist and poet Sir Walter Scott, who wrote his 30 'Waverley novels' there. These were romantic tales of knights and ladies, set in the Scottish Borders.

F

E

D

C

B

A

Lothian

▼ Pigeon castle
Lothian has several doocots, or dovecots, where people bred rock doves (pigeons) for eggs and meat. This doocot at West Saltoun looks like a miniature, turreted castle!

▼ Firth of Forth

LOTHIAN IS MADE UP OF THE HISTORIC counties of West Lothian, Midlothian and East Lothian. The region makes up only about two percent of Scotland's total area, but almost 30 percent of the country's population live there, mostly in the city of Edinburgh.

Lothian, which forms part of the Central Lowlands of Scotland, is bordered by moorland hills. To the southwest are the Pentland Hills, the highest part of which is Scald Law (580 metres). To the southeast are the Moorfoot and Lammermuir Hills, many of which are long-extinct volcanoes. The highest point is Blackhope Scar (650 metres). Four main rivers drain the region – the Almond, the Tyne, the Esk and the Water of Leith.

▼ Bass Rock
Just off the coast of East Lothian, this 107-metre-high rock is the plug of a long-extinct volcano.

Towns, transport and industry

Two huge bridges near Edinburgh, the Forth Rail Bridge and the Forth Road Bridge, link Lothian with the north bank of the river Forth. Besides Edinburgh, the region's largest towns are Livingston, Musselburgh, Bathgate, Whitburn, Penicuick and Dalkeith. In 1962 Livingston was a village with a population of only 2,000. It was designated as a 'new town' in that year, and by 1991 it had over 41,000 inhabitants. There are firms producing electronics and other technological products at Dalkeith and Livingston, but most of the region's industry is concentrated in Edinburgh.

▲ Seaweed

▼ Circuit board
There are electronics companies in and around Dalkeith.

◀ Threshing grain
Andrew Meikle was a millwright at Houston Mill, near Dunbar. In 1788 he patented a brand-new threshing machine that removed wheat and grain from their husks, or chaff.

Farming and wildlife

Arable farming and market gardening are extensive in Lothian. Farmers raise sheep in the Lammermuir Hills, as well as cattle and chickens. Seabird colonies thrive on the Bass Rock, North Berwick Law and other islands in the Firth of Forth, and in a reserve at Aberlady Bay. The Isle of May, in the mouth of the Firth, is used as a stopover by small migrating birds, such as goldcrests, as well as by seabirds. Seals breed on the island, too.

▲ Goldcrest

EAST LOTHIAN
Area: 677 sq km
Population: 85,840
Administrative centre: Haddington

MIDLOTHIAN
Area: 356 sq km
Population: 79,910
Administrative centre: Dalkeith

WEST LOTHIAN
Area: 425 sq km
Population: 146,730
Administrative centre: Livingston

CITY OF EDINBURGH
Area: 262 sq km
Population: 420,170

NORTH SEA

▲ **Roofless ruins**
Linlithgow Palace, where Mary, Queen of Scots was born in 1542, was a favourite residence of Scottish kings. West Lothian used to be called Linlithgowshire.

LOTHIAN'S CASTLES

The region has several notable castles besides Edinburgh Castle. In 1339 the Countess of March and Dunbar, known as Black Agnes, successfully defended Dunbar Castle against a siege. Hailes Castle was reduced to ruins by Oliver Cromwell during the English Civil War. Crichton Castle was begun in the 1400s and enlarged in the 1500s. Tantallon Castle, which was owned by the Douglas family, is a cliff-top stronghold that juts into the North Sea.

▼ **Black Agnes defends Dunbar**

BRILLIANT BRIDGE

The Forth Rail Bridge was completed in 1890 after seven years' work and the loss of 60 workers' lives. The bridge's intricate, iron girders take three years to repaint. Nearby is the Forth Road Suspension Bridge, completed in 1964.

Strathclyde

◀ Bottlenose dolphin
The Isle of Mull is a good place for spotting marine mammals such as minke whales, bottlenose dolphins and seals.

▼ Isle of Mull
The tiny settlement of Calgary is built on a small, secluded bay on the northwest corner of the island.

T HE KINGDOM OF STRATHCLYDE covered southwest Scotland and northwest England about 1,000 years ago. The name was revived in 1975 for the new region of Strathclyde. Modern Strathclyde, which is Scotland's most densely-populated region, is dominated by the city of Glasgow.

In the northwest of Strathclyde there are sea lochs, peninsulas and islands, including part of the Inner Hebrides and the islands of Arran and Mull. The rest of Strathclyde is hilly and includes parts of the Central Lowlands, the Highlands to the north and the Southern Uplands to the south. The river Clyde flows through the Central Lowlands in a great curve, stretching for 170 kilometres from the Lowther Hills to Dumbarton. The Firth of Clyde completes the horseshoe shape.

Coll

Tiree

Staffa

Iona

Colonsa

▲ Dunoon, Argyll
This seaside resort is on the northwestern shore of the Firth of Clyde.

ATLANTIC OCEAN

Water world

◀ Peregrine falcon

Many of the lochs of Argyll and Bute are sea lochs or inlets, such as the Gare Loch and Lochs Long, Fyne, Goil, Gilp, Craignish and Melfort. Loch Linnhe in the north is the start of the Great Glen that crosses the Highland Region. Of the landlocked lochs, the largest are Loch Lomond – which forms most of the boundary with Stirling – Loch Awe and Loch Etive. Fast-flowing streams from the mountains feed these lochs. The name Argyll comes from the Gaelic *Earraghaidheal* which means 'coastland of the Gael.'

Is

Port Ellen●

▼ Sir Walter Scott
Scott's statue looks out across the city of Glasgow from a 24-metre-high column in George Square.

Glasgow City

The Celtic for Glasgow, *Glas Ghu*, or the 'Green Glen,' refers to the valley where most of the city lies. The city straddles the river Clyde, with most business and industry on the north bank. Glasgow's heavy industries developed in the 1800s, but by the 1970s most had closed down. Today the city is a major trading and administrative centre. It has a university, an airport and good transport links to England, Edinburgh and the north of Scotland. Glasgow has a busy port and the banks of the Clyde are lined with docks, quays and shipyards.

▼ Fingal's Cave
This amazing cave on the uninhabited Isle of Staffa inspired composer Felix Mendelssohn to write his *Hebrides Overture*.

▼ **Wild goat**

COUNTY FACTS

ARGYLL AND BUTE
Area: 6,930 sq km
Population: 90,550
Administrative centre:
Lochgilphead
Other key places: Campbeltown,
Dunoon, Inverary, Oban,
Port Ellen

EAST AYRSHIRE
Area: 1,252 sq km
Population: 124,000
Administrative centre:
Kilmarnock

EAST DUNBARTONSHIRE
Area: 172 sq km
Population: 110,220
Administrative centre:
Kirkintilloch

EAST RENFREWSHIRE
Area: 173 sq km
Population: 86,780
Administrative centre: Glasgow

INVERCLYDE
Area: 162 sq km
Population: 89,990
Administrative centre:
Greenock
Other key places: Gourock

NORTH AYRSHIRE
Area: 884 sq km
Population: 139,000
Administrative centre: Irvine
Other key places: Ardrossan,
Brodick

NORTH LANARKSHIRE
Area: 474 sq km
Population: 326,700
Administrative centre:
Motherwell
Other key places: Coatbridge

RENFREWSHIRE
Area: 261 sq km
Population: 177,000
Administrative centre: Paisley

SOUTH AYRSHIRE
Area: 1,202 sq km
Population: 114,000
Administrative centre: Ayr
Other key places: Alloway,
Ballantrae, Girvan

SOUTH LANARKSHIRE
Area: 1,771 sq km
Population: 307,100
Administrative centre: Hamilton
Other key places: Blantyre,
Kirkfieldbank, Lanark

WEST DUMBARTONSHIRE
Area: 162 sq km
Population: 97,790
Administrative centre:
Dumbarton

CITY OF GLASGOW
Area: 175 sq km
Population: 623,850

Mull

Firth of Lorne

Jura

Sound of Jura

KINTYRE

Campbeltown

Mull of Kintyre

NORTH CHANNEL

Dunstaffnage Castle

Oban

Orchy

KILMARTIN VALLEY

Inverary Castle

Inverary

Lochgilphead

Argyll Forest Park

Dunoon

Bute

Arran

Firth of Clyde

Ardrossan

Irvine

Ayr

Girvan

Ballantrae

Stinchar

Doon

Gare Loch

Loch Lomond

Greenock

Dumbarton

Glasgow Airport

Paisley

Kirkintilloch

Glasgow Cathedral

Glasgow

Motherwell

Hamilton

Clyde

Lanark

LOWTHER HILLS

▼ **Jet-skier**

LOCH LOMOND
This is the largest inland waterway in
Britain. There are 37 islands located in the
loch. Today, it is a popular destination
for holidaymakers. Long ago, the islands
provided hideouts for Christian monks.

G

F

E

D

C

B

A

7 6 5 4 3 2 1

▲ Burns Monument
This monument stands in Alloway, Ayrshire, which was the birthplace of Robert Burns. Scots celebrate the poet's birthday each January 25th (Burns Night), with feasting and poetry readings.

THERE WAS A PREHISTORIC SETTLEMENT on the site of modern Glasgow, but the city began to develop only after St Kentigern (also called St Mungo) founded a chapel there in AD543. He died at Glasgow. Argyll had been colonized by Celtish people (known as Scots) from Ireland (known as Scotia). The Scottish king, Kenneth MacAlpin, who ruled from 843 until 860, also reigned over the Picts of northern Scotland. The southern part of the region formed the kingdom of Strathclyde, whose people were ancient Britons. Their king, Malcolm II, ruled from 997 until 1005 and was the first king of all Scotland.

◀ St Mungo's Museum
Opened in 1993, St Mungo's Museum, Glasgow, has a collection of art related to world religions. There is a stunning Zen garden in the museum grounds.

▼ Scottish heroine
Flora MacDonald helped Bonnie Prince Charlie to escape Scotland after the Jacobite Rebellion in the 1700s. She disguised the Stuart prince as a maid for the journey. MacDonald's punishment was imprisonment in Dunstaffnage Castle on the shores of Loch Etive.

Castles
There has been a castle at Dumbarton since the 6th century, sited on a huge rock overlooking the river Clyde. Work on the castle at Rothesay, on the Isle of Bute, first began in the 1100s. The Vikings besieged the castle twice. The present building was largely rebuilt in the 1800s. Bothwell Castle was fought over by English and Scots, part of it being demolished in 1337.

◀ Paisley patterns
The town of Paisley, now in the suburbs of Glasgow, is famed for its patterned fabric. The swirling designs were copied from Indian Mughal art. Paisley became very popular in the 1960s.

▲ David Livingstone
This famous explorer and missionary was born in Blantyre, Lanarkshire. The first Westerner to visit central Africa, he named Victoria Falls after his queen.

▼ Campbell's castle
Archibald Campbell became Duke of Argyll in 1743. He rebuilt the family seat, Inverary Castle, and filled it with collections of books, porcelain and weaponry.

TOIL AND TROUBLE
One of Shakespeare's most famous tragedies is *Macbeth*. The 'Scottish play' tells how Macbeth, one of King Duncan's generals, kills Duncan to become king himself. Three witches that Macbeth met had foretold that he would be king. The real Macbeth died in 1057 and is said to lie buried on Iona.

Famous buildings

Inverary Castle, the seat of the dukes of Argyll, is a large house that was built in the late 1700s. It was designed to look like a French château. Culzean Castle in Ayrshire, another big house, was designed by Robert Adam. Hill House at Helensburgh was designed by Charles Rennie Mackintosh in 1902. Glasgow Cathedral, which dates from 1200, contains the remains of St Kentigern, and is dedicated to him under his nickname of St Mungo.

CAN YOU FIND?

1 Dunstaffnage Castle
2 Glasgow Cathedral
3 Iona
4 Loch Lomond
5 Paisley
6 Staffa

see page 79

▼ Glasgow School of Art
This building was designed inside and out by the architect Charles Rennie Mackintosh in the 1890s. Mackintosh's functional, geometric style is known as Art Nouveau.

Industry

Glasgow and the towns near it along the river Clyde make up Scotland's industrial heartland. The industries located there include shipbuilding, aircraft construction, iron and steel manufacture, and a wide variety of light engineering, especially in the 'new towns' of Cumbernauld, East Kilbride and Irvine. There are whisky distilleries in the region, for example on the Hebridean islands of Islay and Jura.

▲ Ayrshire dairy cattle

Farming

Agriculture plays a small part in the economy of Strathclyde. Farmers raise cattle and sheep, and there is a flourishing line of market gardening.

Central Scotland

THE CENTRAL REGION OF SCOTLAND is made up the geographical counties of Stirlingshire, Clackmannanshire and part of Perthshire. Several important battles between the Scots and the English took place in this region, including the Battle of Bannockburn in 1314.

▼ Lomond's shore
Scotland's largest lake, Loch Lomond, forms the boundary between the Central and Strathclyde regions.

The region lies between the Highlands and the Lowlands. In the north are seven mountains reaching to heights of 900 metres or more. The highest area in the south is the Campsie Fells, made up of extinct, eroded volcanoes. To the east of Loch Lomond, along the southern fringes of the Highlands, lies the scenic Queen Elizabeth Forest, which includes the peak of Ben Lomond and six picturesque lochs.

▲ Fruity folly
When this carved stone folly was built at Dunmore Park, Stirlingshire, in 1761, the pineapple was a rare luxury. Today, the building is let to holidaymakers.

Towns and buildings

The region's main settlement is Stirling, crisscrossed by the river Forth. Overlooking the river and the city centre, on a nearby hill, is the tower built as a national monument to the medieval Scottish hero Sir William Wallace. On another hill stands Stirling Castle, which was captured by Wallace in 1297. The castle has been altered many times since it was built in the 13th century. In the north of the region is Finlarig Castle, built by the Campbell clan.

▼ The Battle of Bannockburn
In 1314 Robert the Bruce led a famous victory against the English at Bannockburn. This won Scotland's independence from England.

▲ The Trossachs
Tourists are attracted to the rugged scenery of Central Scotland. The glen between Lochs Achray and Katrine is known as the Trossachs.

Industry and farming

Most of the region's industry is based in the south. Grangemouth, on the Firth of Forth near Falkirk, has a large oil refinery. Nearby factories produce a wide range of manufactured goods. Whisky distilling and brewing are also important in the area. Farmers in the north of the region rear sheep; in the south, where the soil is better, crops are grown.

COUNTY FACTS

CLACKMANNANSHIRE
Area: 2,196 sq km
Population: 81,630
Administrative centre: Alloa
Other key places: Clackmannan

FALKIRK
Area: 299 sq km
Population: 142,610
Administrative centre: Falkirk
Other key places: Grangemouth

STIRLINGSHIRE
Area: 2,196 sq km
Population: 81,630
Administrative centre: Stirling
Other key places: Bannockburn, Dunblane

Moments in history

Stone Age people once lived on the banks of the river Forth. In AD141 the Romans built a wall across the region to mark the northern border of the mighty Roman Empire. It was called the Antonine Wall, after Emperor Antoninus Pius who ordered its construction. You can see remains of the wall near Falkirk.

Finlarig Castle
Queen Elizabeth Forest Park
▲ Ben Lomond
Teith
Forth
Loch Lomond
CAMPSIE FELLS
Stirling Castle
Stirling
Dunmore Park
Grangemouth
Falkirk

▲ Scottish thistle

▲ Remains of the Antonine Wall

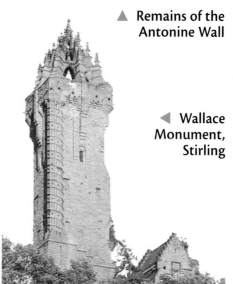
◄ Wallace Monument, Stirling

◄ **Castle Campbell**
This castle near Dollar, Clackmannanshire, dates to the 1400s. It was nicknamed 'Castle Gloom.'

WILLIAM WALLACE

Sir William Wallace is one of Scotland's great heroes. In the late 1200s he led the fight for Scottish independence from England. In 1297 he scored a victory at Stirling Bridge, but he was defeated at Falkirk the following year and escaped to France. On his return to Scotland he was betrayed to the English, and was hung, drawn and quartered, without trial, for the crime of treason. A monument to Wallace was built at Stirling in the 1800s.

Tayside and Fife

▼ River Tay

T HE MIGHTY RIVER TAY, the longest river in Scotland, dominates the region of Tayside and Fife. It flows through an area of rich, fertile farmland. The region includes the historic town of St Andrews, home to Scotland's oldest university and the most famous golf course in the world.

The river Tay, which flows across the region and out into the sea in the Firth of Tay, contains more water than any other river in the British Isles. The north and west of Tayside are mountainous, with the Grampian Mountains over in the northwest. There are several large lakes in the region, including Lochs Rannoch, Tummel, Tay and Leven. The land is flat and fertile in the south. Fife stretches out into the North Sea as a peninsula between the Firths of Tay and Forth.

▲ Time for tee
The rules of golf were first drawn up in the clubhouse at St Andrews in 1754.

Towns and industry

Dundee is the largest city in the region. It is an important engineering centre. Dundee is also famous for its marmalade and jam, but journalism is the biggest employer. Farther west, the city of Perth was once the capital of Scotland. This is an important farming area, and cattle rearing was widespread before the mad cow disease panic of the 1990s. Soft fruits are grown in the area, which is known for its raspberries and tayberries. There is fishing on the south coast, with the port of Arbroath famed for its 'smokies' (smoked haddock).

▲ Culross
In the 1600s, the village of Culross was an important trade centre for salt and coal. Today, it is a perfectly-preserved Scottish burgh with beautiful, painted cottages.

 ▼ Scone
In AD838, Kenneth MacAlpin brought the Stone of Destiny to Scone, near Perth. Scottish kings were crowned on the Stone until the English carried it off in 1297.

Moments in history

In the Middle Ages, Scotland's parliament met at Perth, which was the home of Scottish kings. During the English Civil War this area was involved in some heavy fighting. Fife became known as a kingdom because it was a separate, Pictish province. As recently as 1975, local people argued hard to keep Fife's own identity.

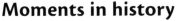

▶ Killicrankie Pass
This stunning gorge is just north of Pitlochry. At the spot called 'Soldiers' Leap,' Bonnie Dundee's Highland soldiers jumped across the Pass in 1689.

COUNTY FACTS

ANGUS
Area: 2,181 sq km
Population: 111,020
Administrative centre: Forfar
Other key places: Arbroath, Montrose

FIFE
Area: 1,323 sq km
Population: 351,200
Administrative centre: Glenrothes
Other key places: Dunfermline, Kirkcaldy, St Andrews

PERTH & KINROSS
Area: 5,311 sq km
Population: 130,470
Administrative centre: Perth
Other key places: Blairgowrie, Crieff

CITY OF DUNDEE
Area: 65 sq km
Population: 153,710

Castles

There are notable castles at Ravenscraig, St Andrews and Claypotts, where the castle is Z-shaped. Mary, Queen of Scots escaped from imprisonment in Loch Leven Castle. Princess Margaret was born at Glamis Castle, Angus, which was the childhood home of Queen Elizabeth, the Queen Mother. Long before her time, the Scottish king Macbeth lived at Glamis in the 11th century.

▼ **Tayberries**

▶ **Paint-a-Pict**
Some of the first people to live in this region were the Picts. Their name means 'painted people.' The Picts were renowned for their painted or tattooed bodies.

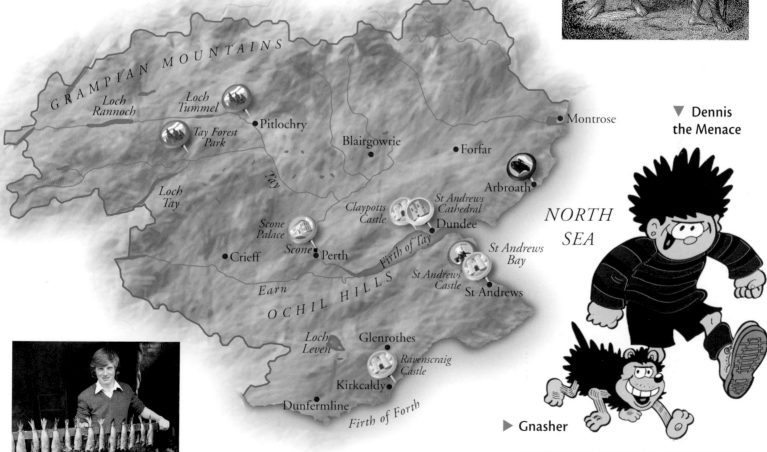

▼ **Dennis the Menace**

▶ **Gnasher**

◀ **In the smokehouse**
Haddock brought in to the port of Arbroath are cured to make the town's famous 'smokies.'

WHAT A MENACE!
DC Thomson employs more people in Dundee than any other business. The company makes many comics, including the world-famous *Beano*.

Grampian

▼ **Speedy Spey**
Well-known for its salmon fishing, the Spey is also the fastest-flowing river in the British Isles.

T HE GRAMPIAN REGION OCCUPIES the northeast corner of Scotland. Grampian includes the old geographical counties of Aberdeenshire, Banffshire, Kincardineshire and most of Morayshire. On the east coast of this mountainous region lies the port of Aberdeen, Scotland's third-largest city and centre of the Scottish oil industry.

▼ **Bred for beef**
The long coat of Highland Cattle protects them from the harsh Scottish winters. The animal produces top-quality beef and is now raised around the world.

The landscape of Grampian is dominated by the rugged Grampian Mountains. Several major rivers cut through this range, including tributaries of the river Spey which, at 172 kilometres long, is second only to the Tay in length and volume of water. Other rivers include the Deveron, Ythan, Don and Dee. The climate of this large region tends to be cool and windy, and snow lies on the mountains for much of the winter. The mountains shelter the rest of the region from the prevailing westerly rain-bearing winds.

Industry
Industry is mostly in the university city of Aberdeen, which lies at the mouth of the river Dee. The city was a bustling port as long ago as Viking times; today, it still has trade links with Scandinavia and the Baltic. Most importantly, though, it is a base for supplying and servicing oil platforms and drilling rigs in the North Sea. Aberdeen, Peterhead (another North-Sea oil centre), Buckie and Fraserburgh are key centres of Scotland's fishing industry. Whisky is distilled in the region, too: the town of Dufftown has seven working distilleries, including the famous Glenfiddich Distillery.

▲ **Granite city**
Robert the Bruce rewarded Aberdeen's loyalty with a Common Good Fund. To this day, money from the fund is spent on beautifying the grey-granite city with dazzling flower displays.

▼ **Tug-o'-war**
Near to the Queen's holiday residence, Balmoral, is the village of Braemar. The Highland Games are held at Braemar every August.

▲ **The oil industry**
Since the oil boom of the 1970s and 1980s, offshore oil rigs have drilled the North Sea for precious supplies of oil.

Farming
Grampian is Scotland's leading farming region, producing barley, oats and wheat. Aberdeen Angus cattle are bred here. There are around 1,000 square kilometres of managed forests.

Moments in history

There are remains of Stone Age and Iron Age peoples across Grampian, including stone circles and hill forts. The region was part of the Pictish kingdom at various times. Celtic missionaries founded monasteries in the area in the 1st millennium AD. Among them was St Machar, an Irish-born bishop who founded the first church in what later became Aberdeen. The present-day twin-towered cathedral of St Machar stands on the site.

NORTH SEA

Buckie • Banff • Fraserburgh • Kinnairds Head
Elgin •
Spey • Keith • Deveron • Turriff • Peterhead
Ythan
Don • Inverurie • Aberdeen Cathedral
Aberdeen Airport
Craigievar Castle
Balmoral Castle • Aberdeen
CAIRNGORM MOUNTAINS • Ballater
Braemar • Dee
GRAMPIAN MOUNTAINS • Dunnottar Castle • Stonehaven

COUNTY FACTS

ABERDEENSHIRE
Area: 6,311 sq km
Population: 223,630
Administrative centre: Aberdeen
Other key places: Braemar, Fraserburgh, Stonehaven

MORAY
Area: 2,238 sq km
Population: 86,250
Administrative centre: Elgin
Other key places: Buckie, Keith

CITY OF ABERDEEN
Area: 186 sq km
Population: 218,220

CASTLES

BALMORAL CASTLE, ABERDEENSHIRE
Rebuilt during the 1800s, this is a private house belonging to the Queen.

CRAIGIEVAR CASTLE, ABERDEENSHIRE
This tall, graceful castle has fairytale towers and turrets of pink granite.

DUNNOTTAR CASTLE, ABERDEENSHIRE
Dunnottar stands on the cliffs near Stonehaven. The Scottish crown and sceptre (known as the 'Honours of Scotland') were hidden here during the English Civil War.

HUNTLY CASTLE, ABERDEENSHIRE
This ruined castle was once home to the Gordon clan. Above the doorway is a carving showing Christ, St Michael and the royal coat of arms.

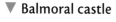
▼ **Balmoral castle**

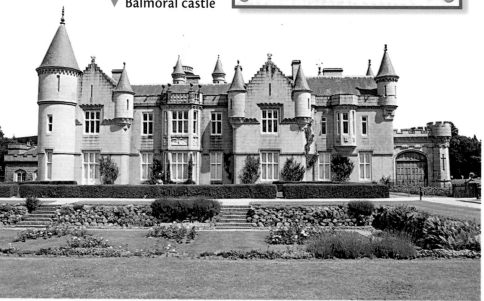

▲ **Barrels of whisky**
The Glenfiddich Distillery produces millions of bottles of single-malt whisky each year. The spirit, made from fermented barley, is aged in oak casks. These are handmade by Glenfiddich's own coopers (barrel-makers).

G

F

E

D

C

B

A

Highland

▼ Ben Nevis
At 1,343 metres, this is the highest peak in the whole British Isles.

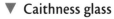

▼ Caithness glass
The glass-blowing factory at Thurso makes beautiful paper-weights and vases.

▼ Monster of the deep
Loch Ness is home of a legendary monster, Nessie. Eyewitnesses describe a creature that looks like a prehistoric plesiosaur.

◀ Plesiosaur

THE HIGHLAND REGION reaches to the northernmost tip of the Scottish mainland at John o'Groats. Although Highland covers a vast area, there are only eight people per square kilometre. It is a region of great beauty, with deep glens, rugged mountains and wild moors.

Most of Highland consists of the Northwest Highlands, plus some lowland areas along the north and east coasts and the Isle of Skye to the west. The mainland part of the region is split by Glen Mor (the Great Glen), a huge fault valley which runs from southwest to northeast. The valley contains a chain of lakes, from the sea loch of Loch Linnhe in the south, continuing with Lochs Lochy, Oich and Ness, and ending at the Moray Firth. The artificial Caledonian Canal links these lochs. Dozens of other lochs are strewn across the region, many opening directly to the sea.

Industry and farming
The region has no major cities: the largest place is the market town of Inverness. The most important industry is manufacturing equipment for the North Sea oil fields. There are aluminium smelters near Fort William and Kinlochleven, and textile mills and whisky distilleries. Apart from sheep-rearing on the hills, there is only limited farming. Large herds of wild deer are culled to provide venison, while fish farms produce salmon.

Moments in history
Around the AD500s the west coast of this region was colonized by Scots from Ireland. Later, Vikings settled in the coastal areas. From about AD1000 Highlanders were organized into clans – families with the same surnames. Sometimes, clan warfare broke out. The last battle on British soil took place in Highland in 1746 – the Battle of Culloden.

▲ Glencoe
This monument marks the events of February 13, 1692. Soldiers from the Campbell clan were staying with the MacDonalds at Glencoe. They slaughtered 38 of their hosts, on the orders of William III.

Portree •
Skye
CUILLIN HILLS
Canna
Rhum
Eigg
Sound of R.....

▶ Dunvesan Castle
Home to the chief clan of Skye, the MacLeods, Dunvesan Castle dates to the 9th century.

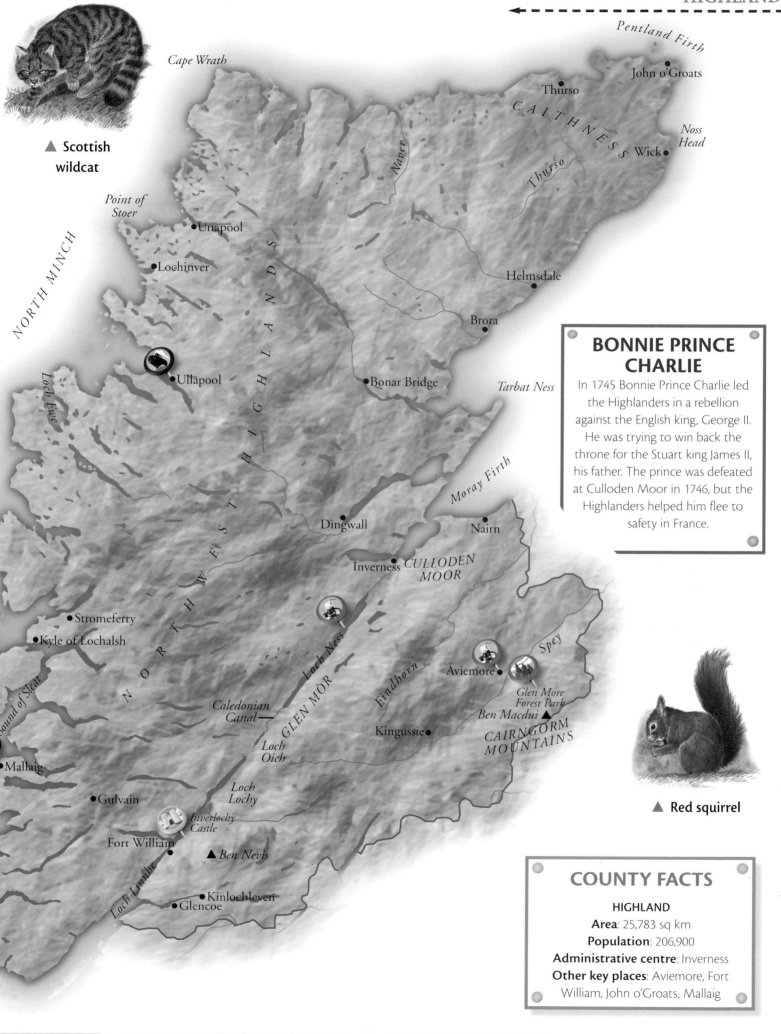

Pentland Firth

John o'Groats

Thurso

Cape Wrath

C A I T H N E S S

Naver

Thurso

Wick

Noss Head

▲ **Scottish wildcat**

Point of Stoer

● Unapool

● Lochinver

Helmsdale ●

N O R T H   M I N C H

Brora ●

Loch Ewe

● Ullapool

● Bonar Bridge

Tarbat Ness

BONNIE PRINCE CHARLIE

In 1745 Bonnie Prince Charlie led the Highlanders in a rebellion against the English king, George II. He was trying to win back the throne for the Stuart king James II, his father. The prince was defeated at Culloden Moor in 1746, but the Highlanders helped him flee to safety in France.

Moray Firth

Dingwall ●

Nairn ●

N O R T H   W E S T   H I G H L A N D S

Inverness ● *CULLODEN MOOR*

● Stromeferry

Spey

● Kyle of Lochalsh

Loch Ness

Aviemore ●

Glen More Forest Park

Sound of Sleat

Findhorn

Caledonian Canal

GLEN MOR

Ben Macdui ▲

CAIRNGORM MOUNTAINS

Kingussie ●

● Mallaig

Loch Oich

▲ **Red squirrel**

● Gulvain

Loch Lochy

Inverlochy Castle

Fort William ●

Ben Nevis ▲

Loch Linnhe

● Kinlochleven

● Glencoe

COUNTY FACTS

HIGHLAND
Area: 25,783 sq km
Population: 206,900
Administrative centre: Inverness
Other key places: Aviemore, Fort William, John o'Groats, Mallaig

7   6   5   4   3   2   1

I

H

G

F

E

D

C

B

A

The Western Isles

There are 54 prehistoric standing stones at Callanish, Lewis. The stones are arranged in the shape of a cross.

THE WESTERN ISLES are a group of islands off the northwest coast of Scotland. They are also known as the Outer Hebrides. Many of the islands are very small and are uninhabited. The largest island is Lewis with Harris (Lewis is the northern part). Regular ferries link the islanders with mainland Scotland. Many inhabitants of the Western Isles still speak Scottish Gaelic as their first language.

To the south of Lewis with Harris are the three islands of North Uist, Benbecula and South Uist, which are linked by bridges. Farther south are Eriskay and Barra, which are reached by a ferry service. There are several smaller islands, including the uninhabited St Kilda group, 64 kilometres to the west. The Western Isles are mostly mountainous, with large areas of open moorland and rolling, grassy plains. Sea lochs indent the craggy coastline, and there are hundreds of small, freshwater lochs inland. A range of hills divides Lewis from Harris, which ends in a long peninsula. The two are connected by a strip of land with a sea loch on either side.

▲ **Black house**
At Eochar, South Uist, you can still find some thatched 'black houses.' Crofters lived in these Viking-style longhouses until the 1930s. Each turf-built house had a central, peat-burning fire but no chimney.

▼ **Whalebones**
At Bragar, on Lewis, two whalebones form an arch by the side of the road. Hanging from the top of the arch is the harpoon used to kill the whale.

Industry and farming

The chief industry of the islands is the production of Harris tweed. Some is manufactured in mills at Stornoway, the chief town, but most is made in the homes of local crofters. There are 5,500 crofts (smallholdings) on the islands, where sheep and cattle are raised and potatoes are grown. Yet less than six percent of the land is suitable for farming. Fishing fleets catch shellfish and a few herrings and whitefish. Tourism and fish farming, mainly of salmon, are growing industries.

▲ **Fishing boats**
At low tide, the islanders' fishing boats are beached on the Island of Lewis.

◀ **Bleak and black**
The landscape of Lewis is dominated by the Black Moor. This peaty moorland is scattered with many tiny lochs.

Moments in history

There are several stone circles in the Western Isles, including Callanish which was begun 4,000 years ago. It is the largest prehistoric monument on the islands and has a central burial chamber. In the 9th century Vikings settled the islands, which were claimed by Norway until 1266. Three clans ruled the islands until after the Jacobite rising of 1745, when they came under the control of the United Kingdom government. Overpopulation and poverty caused many islanders to emigrate to America and Australia in the 1800s.

▼ **Seilebost, Island of Harris**
Tourists are attracted to the islands' stunning white-sand beaches, which rival any in the Caribbean. Unfortunately, the weather does not!

Butt of Lewis

H

Callanish
Stornoway
Eye Peninsula

G

Lewis

ATLANTIC OCEAN

North Minch

E

ST KILDA

Harris

COUNTY FACTS

COUNCIL OF THE WESTERN ISLES (COMHAIRLE NAN EILEAN SIAR)
Area: 3,134 sq km
Population: 29,410
Administrative centre: Stornoway
Other key places: Callanish

North Uist

D

Benbecula

Little Minch

C

▼ **Harris tweed**

South Uist

GIFT TO A GOD
During the 1600s, islanders on Lewis made sure to perform this special rite on October 31st each year. Someone would wade into the sea, chanting to call up the sea god, Shony. They offered the god a cup of ale in the hope of a good crop of seaweed. They used seaweed to fertilize their fields.

B

Kisimul Castle
Barra
SEA OF THE HEBRIDES

A

Orkney

▼ Prepare to dive
Scapa Flow is Europe's best diving site. Wrecks in the clear waters include three German battleships, sunk during World War I, and HMS *Royal Oak*, sunk during World War II.

T HE ORKNEY ISLANDS LIE TEN KILOMETRES from the northeastern tip of mainland Scotland. The Orkney chain contains about 90 islands – as well as numerous holms (islets) and skerries (rocky reefs) – but only 21 of the islands are inhabited. Together with the Shetland Islands, the Orkneys make up the boundary between the North Sea and the Atlantic Ocean.

▲ Bird-watchers' paradise
Steep cliffs on the tiny island of Copinsay provide nesting nooks for many types of seabird, including guillemots (*above*) and kittiwakes.

The Orkneys are separated from Scotland's north coast by a narrow channel called the Pentland Firth. There are steep cliffs on the west and south coasts of the islands, while the north and east coasts are jagged. Inland, the landscape is mostly low-lying, with rocks, swamps and small lochs. Much of the ground is peat-based, but there is some rich arable land. The climate is mild, with plenty of rainfall.

◀ Old Man of Hoy
This spectacular rock stack towers up to a height of 137 metres.

Important places

The largest island, Mainland, has two towns: Kirkwall, the capital, and the port of Stromness. The second-largest island is Hoy, which is part of a group called the South Isles. Off its rugged cliffs stands a detached rocky pillar known as the Old Man of Hoy. To the south, the islands of Burray and South Ronaldsay are linked to Mainland by causeways known as the Churchill Barriers. They were built during World War II to protect the waters of Scapa Flow, which were used by the Royal Navy.

▼ Prehistoric grave
Built around 2750BC, Maes Howe was designed so the Sun's rays shone into the central chamber at the winter solstice. Vikings plundered the site and you can still see their runic graffiti on the chamber walls!

▼ Ring of Brodgar
This 91-metre-wide circle of standing stones was erected on Mainland during the Bronze Age. Thirty-six of the original 60 stones reach skywards to this day.

Industry and farming

Fishing, farming and craft industries are the main occupations of the Orkneys. The chief agricultural products are beef, dairy products, eggs and barley. Barley is malted at the Highland Park Distillery, Kirkwall, to make single-malt whisky. There is a North-Sea oil terminal on the island of Flotta. Air and sea services link the islands, and connect them with Shetland and the mainland of Scotland.

▲ **School air-bus**
Kirkwall airport operates a daily link to the Scottish mainland. Orcadian children have to take the plane to and from school!

Moments in history

Stone Age and Bronze Age peoples lived in Orkney, and they have left behind stone circles, underground houses and standing stones. The Romans knew the islands as the Orcades. Denmark owned the Orkney Islands from the AD800s until 1472. In that year the Scottish king, James III, married a Danish princess and the islands, along with the Shetlands, formed part of her marriage dowry.

Map labels: Westray, North Ronaldsay, Sanday, Rousay, Stronsay, Mainland, Skara Brae, Kirkwall Cathedral, Shapinsay, Stromness, Kirkwall, NORTH SEA, Scapa Flow, Hoy, South Ronaldsay, Pentland Firth

COUNTY FACTS

ORKNEY
Area: 992 sq km
Population: 19,760
Administrative centre: Kirkwall
Other key places: Stromness

SKARA BRAE

Skara Brae is a 5,000-year-old village on Mainland. It was preserved under sand from 2500BC, until a storm revealed it again in 1851. The walls of the huts – and the furniture, too – were built of stone slabs, because the Orkneys have few trees. By examining the remains, experts now know that the villagers grew barley and wheat, and raised cattle and sheep. They also caught seafood and hunted wild game.

▲ **Leatherback turtles**

Shetland

▼ Shetland pony
The world's smallest breed of horse, the Shetland pony, stands just over a metre tall.

▼ Muckle Flugga lighthouse, Unst
David Stevenson built Britain's most northerly lighthouse in 1854. His nephew, author Robert Louis Stevenson, stayed here to write his famous novel *Treasure Island*.

THE SHETLAND ISLANDS (also known as Zetland) are the most northerly part of the British Isles. They lie 80 kilometres northeast of Orkney, and nearly 200 kilometres off the Scottish mainland. The nearest mainland town is Bergen, in Norway.

There are about 100 islands and islets, but less than 20 of them are inhabited. The largest island is Mainland, where more than half the people live. The other large islands are Yell, Unst, Feltar, Whalsay and Bressay. Fair Isle lies 40 kilometres south of the main group. Only about 100 people live there. Shetland is bleak, consisting mostly of moorland with few trees. The coasts are rocky, and are broken up by long sea lochs called 'voes.' The highest point is Ronas Hill (450 metres) on Mainland. The climate is humid and fairly mild, but the weather is always windy and there are often gales.

▼ Sullom Voe
This massive oil terminal is Europe's biggest. Two 160-km-long underwater pipelines carry crude oil there from the North-Sea oilfields.

Industry

North Sea oil has brought much-needed work to the Shetlanders. There is a huge oil terminal at Sullom Voe. Sumburgh Airport, on the southern tip of Mainland, operates a helicopter service out to the oil rigs, as well as services to the mainland cities of Aberdeen and Inverness.

▼ Ness Yole
This boat used for inshore fishing shows the influence of the Vikings, or Norsemen. Shetland was part of Norway from the 800s to the 1400s.

▼ Fair Isle tank top
An authentic Fair Isle knit must have been made on Fair Isle itself and have the distinctive OXOXO patterning.

Farming

Agriculture in Shetland is limited because of poor soil and rugged land. Most farmers work on crofts (smallholdings) and rear sheep. Shetland sheep produce fine-quality wool which is hand-knitted by the islanders. Hardy Shetland ponies are reared on Unst and some of the other islands. Fishing boats bring in catches of herring and whitefish to the ports of Lerwick and Scalloway. Fish farming is a growing industry.

<------------------------

COUNTY FACTS

SHETLAND
Area: 1,438 sq km
Population: 22,830
Administrative centre: Lerwick
Other key places: Scalloway

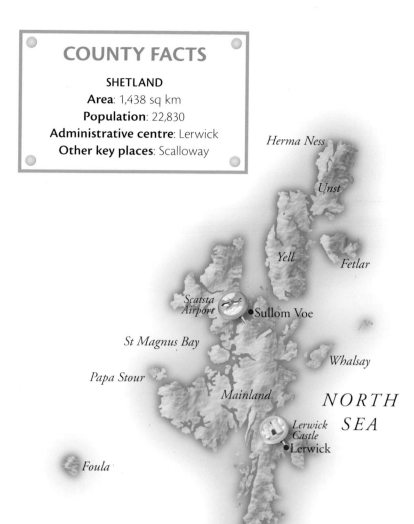

Herma Ness

Unst

Yell

Fetlar

Scatsta
Airport

Sullom Voe

St Magnus Bay

Whalsay

Papa Stour

Mainland

*NORTH
SEA*

Lerwick
Castle
Lerwick

Foula

Fair Isle

Moments in history

The earliest inhabitants of the Shetland Islands were prehistoric, and they have left behind many remains, including stone circles. The site of Jarlshof, in the south of Mainland, shows signs of continuous settlement over several centuries. There is a group of Bronze Age houses which were built in the 700s BC. Viking settlers arrived in the 8th century AD, and most Shetlanders today are of Norse descent. The islands belonged to Norway until 1472, when they were annexed to Scotland along with the Orkneys.

▲ **Jarlshof**
This prehistoric and Viking settlement was uncovered by a gale in the early 1900s.

▼**Up-Helly-Aa**

FESTIVAL OF FIRE

On the last Tuesday of January each year, Shetlanders remember their Norse past by celebrating the festival of Up-Helly-Aa. Groups of men dress up as Vikings and parade through the streets of Lerwick. They pull a specially-built Viking galley, with a carved dragon prow, down to the water's edge. There it is launched and set on fire. In Viking times, the bodies of dead chiefs were pushed out to sea in blazing longboats.

H

G

F

E

D

C

B

A

Ireland

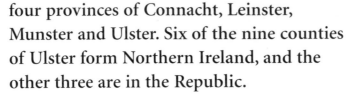

◀ Shamrock
The shamrock, or wood sorrel, is Ireland's national flower.

◀ Irish harp
The Irish harp, around since medieval times, is often used as a symbol of the country itself.

I RELAND IS THE SECOND-LARGEST ISLAND of the British Isles. Its southern part forms the Republic of Ireland. The northeast corner is the province of Northern Ireland, which is part of the United Kingdom. Historically, Ireland was divided into the four provinces of Connacht, Leinster, Munster and Ulster. Six of the nine counties of Ulster form Northern Ireland, and the other three are in the Republic.

ATLANTIC OCEAN

IRISH SEA

▲ Patron saint of Ireland
The feast day of Ireland's patron saint, St Patrick, falls on March 17th. On that day, Irish people wear green, their national colour.

In its early days Ireland was torn by wars between rival kings, whom Viking settlers were unable to control. In 1166 the king of Leinster, Dermot MacMurrough, travelled to Wales and appealed to a Norman baron, nicknamed Strongbow, for help against his enemies. Strongbow married Dermot's daughter, and in 1171 succeeded him as king of Leinster. Strongbow in turn appealed for help to the English king, Henry II. Henry tried to conquer the country. Seven centuries of struggle followed, culminating in the 1801 Act of Union which made Ireland part of the United Kingdom.

▼ British soldiers
From 1972, British soldiers were posted in Northern Ireland to help the police to control terrorism.

Struggle for freedom

The 19th century was a time of great poverty and hardship in Ireland. Increasingly the Irish demanded Home Rule. Although this was promised, it was postponed because of World War I. Beginning in 1916, the Irish people took power by force, and won some independence in 1922. Nearly all the Irish were Roman Catholics. The Protestant majority in the northeast chose to remain part of the United Kingdom. Southern Ireland was at first a Free State, with the British monarch as its nominal head of state. In 1949 it declared itself an independent republic, with the name of Eire, the Gaelic for Ireland.

The Republic of Ireland

The Republic of Ireland's government consists of a president, a parliament with two houses, a prime minister and a cabinet. The president is head of state, with mainly ceremonial duties. The parliament consists of an upper house and a lower house, called Dáil Éireann. The Dáil, the main law-making body, has 166 elected members. Parliament meets in Leinster House. Local government is in the hands of 27 county councils.

◄ **Roman Catholicism**
The Republic of Ireland's official religion is Roman Catholicism. Believers buy candles and light them in church as an offering to God.

Northern Ireland

Northern Ireland is a province of the United Kingdom. It had its own parliament and administration, founded in 1921, but sections of the population did not want to remain part of the United Kingdom. In 1969 the Provisional IRA (Irish Republican Army) began a terrorist campaign with the aim of Northern Ireland joining the Republic.

To maintain control, the British government suspended the Northern Ireland Parliament, and began to rule the province directly from Westminster. Much of the life of the province divided along religious lines, with the Roman Catholic minority in opposition to the Protestant majority. Although most ordinary people wished to live in peace, some sections of both communities formed paramilitary organizations in violent opposition to the British government and its policies.

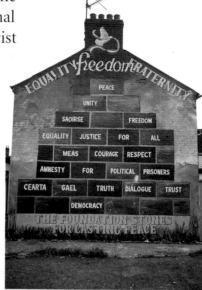

▲ **Political slogans**
The buildings of Belfast bear the mark of decades of political unrest, with many slogans and murals.

COUNTRY FACTS

NORTHERN IRELAND
Area: 14,121 sq km
Population: 1,595,000
Capital: Belfast
Other cities: Bangor, Londonderry (Derry), Newtownabbey
Official language: English
Main religions: Protestantism, Roman Catholicism
Currency: Pound sterling (£)
Highest point: Slieve Donard (852 m)
Longest river: Upper and Lower Bann (137 km)
Largest lake: Lough Neagh (396 sq km)

REPUBLIC OF IRELAND
Area: 70,284 sq km
Population: 3,590,000
Capital: Dublin
Major cities: Cork, Dún Laoghaire, Limerick, Waterford
Official languages: English, Irish Gaelic
Main religions: Roman Catholicism, Protestantism
Currency: Punt (Euro from year 2002)
Highest point: Carrauntoohill (1,041 m)
Longest river: Shannon (370 km)
Largest lake: Lough Corrib (176 sq km)

CUCHULAIN

To this day, poets are inspired by the myths of Ireland, which include tales of many great heroes. Cuchulain was one, said to have lived during the 1st century BC. He was the son of the god Lug, and a fierce warrior. His strength was superhuman and even the most vile monsters ran away from him! According to legend, he defeated whole armies single-handed – including that of Queen Maeve of Connacht when he was just 17 years old. Cuchulain was as handsome as he was brave, but he easily flew into a rage. He is said to have died, aged 27, after being tricked by his enemies.

The road to peace

In 1985 the Dublin and Westminster governments signed an Anglo-Irish agreement, giving the Irish government an advisory role in Northern Ireland's affairs. Fresh efforts to reach a settlement began in 1997, and in 1998 the Republican and Loyalist organizations agreed to stop violence. In 1998 Roman Catholic and Protestant members were elected to a new assembly, with a view to forming a new government for the province.

Ireland
Physical features

IRELAND IS SEPARATED FROM GREAT BRITAIN by the Irish Sea. At Torr Head, County Antrim, Ireland is only 22 kilometres away from the Mull of Kintyre in Scotland. The main features of Ireland's landscape are its rolling plains, its mountains and its coastline. Ireland is often called the 'Emerald Isle' because of its wide expanses of picturesque green lowland.

▲ **Northern pike**
Ireland's rivers and lakes are home to salmon, trout, pike, bream, perch and roach.

The centre of the island is a broad, low plain, which consists mostly of farmland with some woodlands and peat bogs. Scattered mountains and highland regions lie near the coasts, notably the Plateau of Antrim and the Mourne Mountains in the northeast, the Donegal Mountains in the northwest, the Wicklow Mountains in the southeast, and the Mountains of Mayo, Connemara and Kerry in the west.

▼ **River Shannon**
The Shannon is edged by marshland for much of its 370-km course. It drains an area of over 15,500 sq km.

▲ **Boggy harvest**
Over many thousands of years, large areas of peat bogs have formed in Ireland. Peat is the rotted remains of ancient vegetation. It is cut and dried to make fuel.

The coastline along the Irish Sea is smooth compared to Ireland's west coast. Pounded by Atlantic waves and storms, the west coast is a mass of deep bays and inlets, with high, rocky cliffs. The river Shannon, the longest in the British Isles, empties into the Atlantic Ocean. The largest of Ireland's many lakes, which are mostly in the west of the island, is Lough Neagh, in Northern Ireland.

▼ **Rocky cliffs**
Donegal, in the northwest of Ireland, faces the powerful Atlantic Ocean. Its dramatic, jagged cliffs have been weathered over millions of years.

Rocks of Ireland

Like Great Britain, Ireland was once part of two separate, ancient continents. If you imagine a diagonal line from Berwick-upon-Tweed, England, to the mouth of the river Shannon, that is where the two continents came together (see pages 68–69). Everything north of the line on both islands was originally part of a continent which continued into North America. A long-vanished ocean separated it from the land that is now England and the southern part of Ireland. As a result, the rocks of Northern Ireland are a continuation of those found in Scotland. The hills of western Galway and Counties Mayo and Londonderry were originally a continuation of the Scottish Highlands.

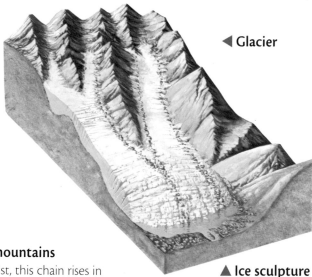

◀ **Glacier**

▲ **Ice sculpture**
Glaciers shaped the Irish landscape during the last Ice Age, 10,000 years ago.

A lot of these hills have a foundation of granite, an igneous (volcanic) rock. The extraordinary rock formation of the Giant's Causeway, County Antrim, is similar to the rock columns at Fingal's Cave, on the island of Staffa in the Inner Hebrides. Both formations were part of the same volcanic eruption. When the hot, liquid rock flooded out of the Earth's interior, it cooled to form amazing six-sided columns, or pillars, of a black rock called basalt.

Cut off by the sea

The Irish Sea formed thousands of years before Great Britain was separated from continental Europe. When animals and plants reached the British Isles from continental Europe, some species did not reach the island of Ireland before it was cut off from Great Britain. Examples include snakes, moles, voles and common shrews.

▲ **Wicklow mountains**
Shrouded in mist, this chain rises in County Wicklow, Leinster. Long ago, glaciers scraped and smoothed the hills, exposing the underlying granite.

▲ **Emerald Isle**
Green is Ireland's national colour. The fields glow green, thanks to plentiful rains brought by the prevailing winds across the Atlantic.

CLIMATE
Ireland's climate is mild and damp and there are few sharp frosts or heavy snowfalls. Its mildness is due to the North Atlantic Drift, a current that brings the warm waters of the Gulf Stream to northwestern Europe. The rains are brought to Ireland by a series of depressions (low-pressure systems) which are carried across the Atlantic by the prevailing winds. Most of the island has 762–1,270 mm of rain a year. The highest rainfall occurs in western Connacht and County Kerry, where it can reach 2,286–2,540 mm. As in England, the sunniest part of the island is the southeastern corner.

▼ **Giant's Causeway**
Some of these rocky, hexagonal pillars of basalt in County Antrim are up to six metres high and half a metre across.

▲ **The Burren**
Rocky outcrops of limestone dot the landscape of the Burren in County Clare. It is home to some unique alpine plants.

Belfast

► **Custom House**
An essential building in any busy port, Belfast's Custom House is on the waterfront.

BELFAST HAS BEEN THE CAPITAL of Northern Ireland since 1920, when the province first became separated from the southern part of the island. It is the largest city in the province, with a population of 296,300. Belfast stands on the river Lagan, at the head of Belfast Lough, a large bay facing towards Scotland. It is a seaport and Northern Ireland's leading industrial centre.

Belfast's linen-weaving is a historic industry. Shipbuilding began in the late 18th century, and is still one of Belfast's main industries. A huge aircraft factory was established in 1937.

Important buildings

Belfast has some fine buildings, many dating from the late 1800s and early 1900s. Others have been built since World War II. (Enemy bombing destroyed much of the city in 1941, with the loss of 1,000 lives.) The heart of the city is Donegall Square, where City Hall stands.

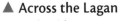

▲ **Across the Lagan**
Queen's Bridge was built by Sir Charles Lanyon. Completed in 1843, it is named after Queen Victoria.

▼ **Shipbuilding**
The ill-fated *Titanic* was made by Belfast shipbuilders. The city's shipyards line the eastern shores of Belfast Lough.

▲ **Belfast Castle**
The castle grounds feature mosaic cats, sculpture and garden furniture. There's a legend that the castle residents will have good luck if a white cat lives there.

Other notable landmarks in the city centre are the Royal Courts of Justice and St Anne's Cathedral. The Ulster Museum is set in the picturesque surroundings of the city's Botanic Gardens. In the eastern suburb of Stormont is Parliament House. The governmental Northern Ireland Office is based in nearby Stormont Castle. Northern Ireland has two universities: Queen's University, which dates from 1908 and is the province's largest; and the University of Ulster, which was formed in 1984 and has campuses in Belfast, Coleraine and Londonderry.

PLACES OF INTEREST

ART GALLERIES
Malone House, Old Museum Arts Centre, Ormeau Baths Gallery

PARKS
Cavehill Country Park,
Lady Dixon Park,
Ormeau Park

PLACES OF WORSHIP
Crescent Church, First Presbyterian Church, Moravian Church, St Anne's Cathedral, St Malachy's. St Mary's, St Matthew's

MUSEUMS
Ulster Museum

OTHER ATTRACTIONS
Albert Memorial Clocktower, Belfast Zoo, Botanic Gardens, Lagan Lookout Visitor Centre

Moments in history

The earliest fact we know about Belfast is that in the 1170s a Norman baron, John de Courci, built a castle by a ford across the river. It became known as Beal Feirste, meaning 'the approach to the crossing.' De Courci conquered Ulster, but his castle did not survive. In 1611 Sir Arthur Chichester, Lord Deputy of Ireland, built a new 'stately palace.' Fire destroyed Chichester's castle in 1708, but the town surrounding it grew and thrived. Belfast's main industry was the spinning and weaving of linen from local-grown flax, and this had expanded in the 1600s following the arrival of French Huguenot (Protestant) refugees, who were expert weavers. By 1800 the city was home to 20,000 people; today, it has a population of over 362,000.

Belfast's recent history has been dominated by political conflict. Street riots during 1969 led to the introduction of British troops in 1972. The rest of the 20th century saw terrorism on both sides, but a Peace Agreement in 1999 provided new hope for the city's future.

▲ **City Hall**
A central landmark is City Hall, Donegall Square. The Renaissance-style building was completed in 1906.

◀ **Glasshouse**
The impressive, iron-framed Palm House, built between 1839 and 1852, is the centrepiece of Belfast's Botanic Gardens.

◀ **Belfast streets**
The cityscape is dominated by rows and rows of terraced houses, and by the river Lagan.

▲ **Stormont Castle**
The Northern Ireland Parliament met at Stormont from 1932 until 1972. There are hopes that the new Northern Ireland Assembly will meet here.

Northern Ireland

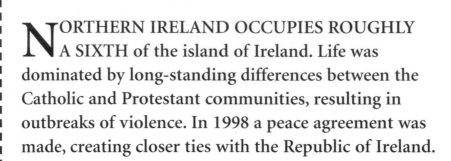

NORTHERN IRELAND OCCUPIES ROUGHLY A SIXTH of the island of Ireland. Life was dominated by long-standing differences between the Catholic and Protestant communities, resulting in outbreaks of violence. In 1998 a peace agreement was made, creating closer ties with the Republic of Ireland.

The landscape is characterized by fertile, rolling plains and low mountain ranges, which are often close to the coastline. In the west, the thinly-populated Sperrin Mountains form a crescent running almost to the sea at Coleraine in the north. In the northeast, the high plateau of the Mountains of Antrim is cut by deep glens. In the southeast, the Mourne Mountains contain the region's highest peak, Slieve Donard (852 metres). Flanking the river Mourne in Tyrone are two hills, Bessy Bell and Mary Gray. They are named after two Scotswomen who died of plague in Perth in 1666.

Lakes and rivers

The region has several freshwater lakes, of which Lough Neagh is the most important. It covers 396 square kilometres and is the largest lake in the British Isles. The longest river is the river Bann, which is really two rivers – the Upper Bann and the Lower Bann. The river Foyle forms part of the western border with the Irish Republic.

Important towns

Two-thirds of the population live in cities and towns. The largest cities are Belfast and Londonderry. Belfast is a university town and Northern Ireland's main seaport, operating ferry services to other ports in Northern Ireland and to the west coasts of England and Scotland. The city also has an international airport.

▼ Stepping stones
According to legend, a giant called Finn MacCool built the Giant's Causeway so that he could walk to Scotland without getting his feet wet! It consists of over 40,000 hexagonal columns of volcanic rock, called basalt.

▼ County Down
The Mourne Mountains are topped with dark, craggy peaks of granite. The beautiful Silent Valley cuts through the mountains.

▲ Sticky trick
This carnivorous plant is native to Ireland's bogs, as found in County Tyrone. It sets a gummy trap for passing insects.

▲ Statue of hope
This monument in Londonderry is called 'Hands across the Divide.' The 1998 peace agreement led to hopes for greater tolerance between Protestants and Catholics.

DODOS & DINOS
The gardens at Mount Stewart House, County Down, are populated by strange statues. They include mermaids, platypuses, dinosaurs and dodos.

COUNTY FACTS

COUNTY ANTRIM
Area: 2,832 sq km
Key places: Antrim, Ballycastle, Ballymena, Bushmills, Carrickfergus

COUNTY ARMAGH
Area: 1,254 sq km
Key places: Armagh, Portadown

BELFAST DISTRICT
Area: 65 sq km
Key place: Belfast

COUNTY DOWN
Area: 2,448 sq km
Adminstrative centre: Downpatrick
Other key places: Banbridge, Bangor, Newry, Newtownards

COUNTY FERMANAGH
Area: 1,676 sq km
Key place: Enniskillen

COUNTY LONDONDERRY
Area: 2,077 sq km
Key places: Coleraine, Limavady, Portstewart

LONDONDERRY CITY DISTRICT
Area: 8.8 sq km
Key place: Londonderry

COUNTY TYRONE
Area: 3,137 sq km
Key places: Cookstown, Dungannon, Omagh

Wildlife havens

Strangford Lough is a naturalists' paradise, with flocks of ducks, geese and wading birds, as well as large numbers of basking seals. Birds of prey, such as buzzards and peregrines, are a regular sight along the northern stretch of coastline known as White Park Bay. Further south, in the Sperrin Mountains, sika deer can be spotted in the Gortin Glen Forest Park. Huge numbers of wildfowl, including great crested grebes, spend their winter in the reedbeds of Lough Neagh.

▲ Reedbed

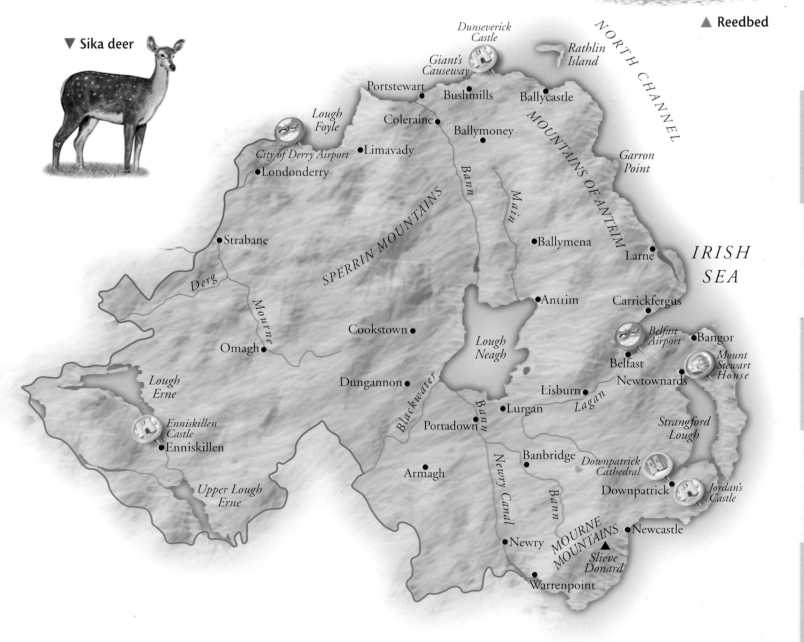

▼ Sika deer

THE EARLIEST INHABITANTS of Northern Ireland were Stone Age people, who left huge burial chambers and large standing stones. For a long time, their burial chambers were believed to be the graves of giants.

▲ **Legananny Dolmen**
This monument in County Down dates back to Stone Age times.

The earliest rulers are mostly legendary ones, but they were probably based on real people. Two thousand years ago there was a Kingdom of Ulster. The ruins of its capital, Emain Macha, lie near present-day Armagh Town. According to legend, the ruler of Ulster was Conor MacNessa, who had an army known as the Knights of the Red Branch. Its greatest warrior was Cuchulain, said to be the son of the sun god Lug. In the AD300s a king named Niall of the Nine Hostages formed a kingdom in the west of Northern Ireland. At about that time many of the region's people were Scots, who later invaded Scotland and settled there.

Protestants in Northern Ireland

The English made several attempts to conquer Northern Ireland, but were fiercely resisted. From 1610 onwards the British rulers began what is called the plantation of Ireland, encouraging English and Scottish people to move there. This introduced a number of Protestants into an island which, until then, had been completely Roman Catholic.

▲ **March of the Orangemen**
In the late 17th century there was a war between the ousted Roman Catholic king, James II of England, and his Protestant successor, William III of Orange. In support of William, the apprentice boys of Londonderry shut the city gates to keep out James's armies. To this day, Protestant political groups, known as Orange Lodges, have celebrated with a marching season that lasts from Easter until July 12th.

PATRON SAINT

St Patrick brought Christianity to Ireland in the 5th century. According to legend, he drove all the snakes from Ireland into the sea. Patrick's grave is said to be in the grounds of Down Cathedral in Downpatrick. Two cathedrals in Armagh City honour the saint: St Patrick's Church of Ireland Cathedral and St Patrick's Roman Catholic Cathedral.

▼ **Ancient prayer book**
The *Antiphonary of Bangor* is a prayer book that dates back to the AD600s. It is all that remains of the monastery at Bangor, County Down, which was sacked by the Vikings and abandoned in the 11th century.

▲ **Making linen**
Huguenot weavers arrived in Northern Ireland in the 1600s and by the 1800s, Belfast was nicknamed Linenopolis. To break down the harvested flax, it was beaten, and then 'scutched' (*left*) with a large knife. Then it was ready to be woven on the loom (*right*).

Castles

Jordan's Castle in County Down was built in the late 1300s and is virtually undamaged. The cliff-top ruins of Dunseverick Castle stand on the north coast of County Antrim. It was once the most fortified castle in the whole of Ireland. The castle was razed by Oliver Cromwell's English soldiers in the 1600s. Nearby is the famous Carrick-a-Rede rope bridge, which links the mainland to a rocky island where there are salmon fisheries. Both Dromore and Clough are motte-and-bailey castles dating from Norman times.

Industry

Light industry, including rayon production, linen weaving and computer manufacture, are among the chief activities in Northern Ireland. There is heavy industry, such as shipbuilding and aircraft manufacture, in and around Belfast. Near Lower Lough Erne is the village of Belleek, famous for its delicate, shiny pottery. A dam near the village provides hydroelectric power. The tiny town of Bushmills in County Antrim is home to the world's oldest distillery.

Farming

Farmers in Northern Ireland export food to the rest of the British Isles. Sheep farming is the main activity in the northeast. In the valley of the river Laggan, between counties Antrim and Down, farmers rear pigs and dairy herds, and grow oats and potatoes.

▲ Potato plant

WHAT'S IN A NAME?

ANTRIM
The Gaelic *Aontroim* means 'one house.'

ARMAGH
This county is named after an Irish warrior goddess, Macha.

COUNTY DOWN
Down is named after the town of Downpatrick, which means 'St Patrick's dún,' or fort.

FERMANAGH
The Gaelic *Fear Manach* means 'district of the monks.'

LONDONDERRY
The original name, Derry, means 'oak wood.' St Columba founded a monastery in a nearby oak grove in AD546. In 1613 Londoners settled there so the name changed to Londonderry.

TYRONE
Tír Eoghain means 'land belonging to Eoghain.' Eoghain was the son of a 5th-century High King of Ireland.

▲ **Whiskey vats**
The Bushmills distillery in County Antrim has been making whiskey since 1608.

CAN YOU FIND?

1 Armagh
2 Belfast
3 Bushmills
4 Downpatrick Cathedral
5 Slieve Donard

see page 103

Dublin

DUBLIN IS THE CAPITAL of the Republic of Ireland. It was founded by the Vikings in the 9th century on a hill overlooking the river Liffey. They called its harbour the Black Pool – in Irish Gaelic, 'dubh linn.' The city's official name now is Baile Atha Cliath – 'Ford of the Hurdles.' Dublin is Ireland's largest city and its leading port. It is famed for its handsome architecture, wide streets and large squares.

Dublin is the centre of Ireland's road and rail networks. Dublin Airport is at Collinstown, to the north of the city. The city's manufacturing industries include chemicals, clothing, electronics, tobacco and brewing. The service sector plays an important part in the city's economy, and Dublin is a major banking and financial centre.

▲ Dublin's bridges
Fourteen bridges span the Liffey in the city, joining the north and south. The river flows through scenic Phoenix Park.

Important buildings

Dublin has many fine buildings. They include Dublin Castle, the nextdoor City Hall, the Four Courts (law courts), the Custom House, the General Post Office and the Abbey Theatre. Some buildings were damaged in the Easter Rising of 1916, and in the Civil War of 1922–3, but they have all been restored. The city's main shopping area lies along and around Grafton Street and O'Connell Street. At 46 metres wide, O'Connell Street is one of the widest in Europe. Christ Church Cathedral was founded in 1038 within the old walls of the city. St Patrick's Cathedral, which is outside the the old city walls, was begun in 1190. Both of these cathedrals are Anglican (Protestant). The Roman Catholic Metropolitan Pro-Cathedral was built in 1816. There are three universities. The University of Dublin, for which only one college was ever completed, is known as Trinity College, Dublin.

▼ Custom House
Flames claimed Dublin's Custom House in 1921, but it has been restored following James Gandon's original design of the 1780s. The copper dome features four clocks and is topped by a statue of Hope.

▲ Government Buildings
Opened in 1911, these buildings contain the Taoiseach's (Prime Minister's) office and the cabinet rooms.

Moments in history

Although the Irish occupied the city several times, it remained principally in Viking hands until 1170, when it was finally captured by Normans from England. Two years later King Henry II made Dublin the centre of his attempted conquest of Ireland. But the conquest was limited, and for centuries the English territory was confined to an area around Dublin, which became known as the English Pale (boundary). Its people were mostly Protestants. In 1649, during the English Civil War, Dublin was captured by the Parliamentary army of Oliver Cromwell. At that time it had a population of 9,000.

During the 1700s Dublin grew and prospered, and by 1800 it was second only to London among the cities of the British Empire. Ireland had its own parliament, based in Dublin in a building that is now the Bank of Ireland. A viceroy represented the British monarch. The Act of Union in 1801 abolished the parliament.

▲ Dublin streets
The Liffey cuts across the city streets down to Portobello Harbour.

◄ Parnell Square
The square's central statue by Oisin Kelly shows the Children of Lir, the Celtic sea god. They represented the powers of evil.

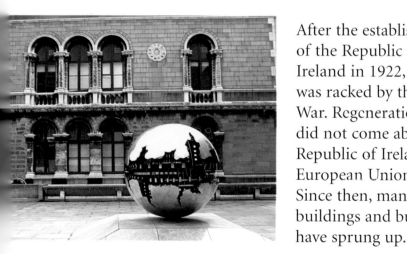

After the establishment of the Republic of Ireland in 1922, Dublin was racked by the Civil War. Regeneration of the city did not come about until the Republic of Ireland joined the European Union in 1973. Since then, many new buildings and businesses have sprung up.

▲ Trinity College
Elizabeth I founded Dublin's university in 1592. Its Old Library houses the *Book of Kells*.

▼ The DART
The Dublin Area Rapid Transport is an overground rail service that links different parts of the city.

PLACES OF INTEREST

ART GALLERIES
City Arts Centre, Irish Museum of Modern Art, Municipal Gallery of Modern Art, National Gallery

PARKS
Phoenix Park, St Stephen's Green

PLACES OF WORSHIP
Christ Church Cathedral, St Mary's Pro-Cathedral, St Patrick's Cathedral

MUSEUMS
Dublin Writers' Museum, Heraldic Museum, Museum of Childhood, National Museum, Natural History Museum, Pearse Museum

OTHER ATTRACTIONS
Dublin Castle, Dublinia, Dublin's Viking Adventure, Dublin Zoo, James Joyce Centre, National Botanic Gardens, National Wax Museum, Trinity College

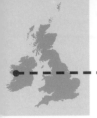

Connacht

▼ A Galway village
Leenane, on Killary
Harbour, is famous for
its woollen industry.
There is even a Sheep
and Wool Museum.

THE ANCIENT KINGDOM of Connacht
lies in the west of Ireland. Its jagged,
mountainous west coast is divided from
the rest of Connacht by a series of lakes.

The Shannon, the longest river in the British Isles,
rises in northern Connacht and forms most of
the border with Leinster to the east. It flows
southwards through a chain of lakes and
out into the Atlantic. Hundreds of small
islands lie off the coast of Connacht.

Galway

Connemara, County Galway, is a
mountainous region of peat bogs and
thousands of small lakes. Part of it is a
national park. Most people in this region live on small
farms. Connemara ponies are bred here, and a form of
limestone known as Connemara marble is mined. To the
east is Lough Corrib, which extends almost to Galway City,
the chief town of the county and an important industrial
centre. The Aran Islands of Inishmore, Inisheer and
Inishmaan are situated in Galway Bay.

▼ Pirate queen
Grace O'Malley was the
daughter of a Connacht
chief – and a notorious
pirate during the 1500s.
She had a fleet of pirate
ships and her own
castle on Clare Island,
County Mayo.

▼ Wicker and tar
A curragh is a tiny Irish
fishing boat. Traditionally it
consists of a wicker frame
that is made watertight
with a covering of leather,
canvas or tar.

Mayo, Sligo and Leitrim

Ireland's largest coastal island, Achill Island, lies to
the south of Blacksod Bay, County Mayo. The island
has a unique blend of sandy beaches, sheer cliffs,
moorland and mountains. Two ranges, Slieve Gamph
and the Ox Mountains, lie on the Mayo-Sligo border.
Ireland's most famous poet, William Butler Yeats, is
buried at Drumcliff in County Sligo, a place which
inspired many of his poems. The northern part of
County Leitrim is mountainous, while further south
are low hills and valleys where the soil is poor.

Connacht and Roscommon

Connacht is farming country, with few
large towns. County Roscommon is
sandwiched between two rivers, the
Shannon to the east and the Suck to
the west. The land is boggy, but there is
good grazing.

◄ Aran jumpers
Older inhabitants of
the Aran Islands still
wear traditional
dress, including
the famous Aran
sweater. And many
still speak Irish Gaelic
as their first language.

COUNTY ROSCOMMON (ROS COMÁIN)
Area: 2,460 sq km
Population: 55,000
Administrative centre:
Roscommon Town
Other key places: Boyle,
Strokestown

COUNTY SLIGO (CONTAE SHLIGIGH)
Area: 1,800 sq km
Population: 56,000
Administrative centre: Sligo City
Other key places: Drumcliff, Easky

Moments in history

Perched on top of a sheer cliff on the Aran island of Inishmore is the spectacular prehistoric hill fort of Dun Aengus. The Aran Islands boast the remains of several forts, dating from the Iron Age through to the Middle Ages. The Kingdom of Connacht rose in importance under Niall of the Nine Hostages, who ruled at Tara, County Meath, from AD380 to 405. As *Árd Rí* (High King), Niall was ruler of all Ireland. His descendants held the title of *Árd Rí* until the Normans from England conquered Connacht in the 1200s.

▲ Dun Aengus

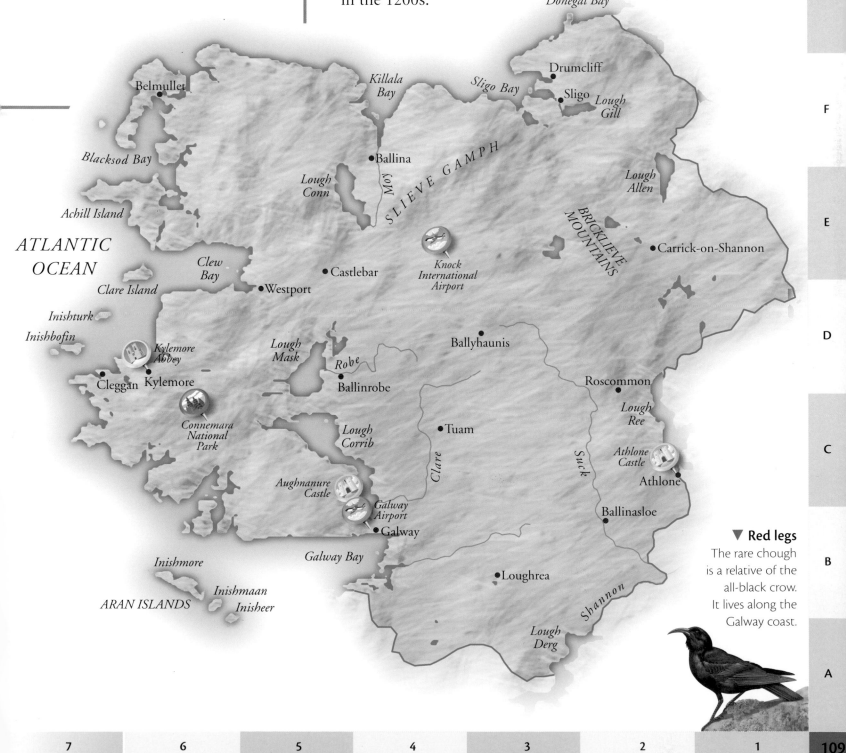

▼ **Red legs**
The rare chough is a relative of the all-black crow. It lives along the Galway coast.

Leinster

L EINSTER IS THE LARGEST of Ireland's four provinces, consisting of a total of 12 counties. The province is famous for horse breeding and horse-racing: races have been held at the world-famous Curragh racecourse in County Kildare for around 2,000 years.

▼ **Fictional village**
The village of Avoca, in southern Wicklow, is the setting for the TV series *Ballykissangel*. Around 70,000 fans of the series make a pilgrimage to Avoca each year.

Leinster is surrounded by Ulster to the north, the Irish Sea to the east, Munster to the south and Connacht to the west. The coastline with the Irish Sea is far less jagged than Ireland's rugged west coast. Carlingford Lough, a long sea inlet, separates Leinster from County Down. Carlingford Mountain (590 metres) rises near the shores of the lough. The chief river of the province is the Liffey, which rises in the Wicklow Mountains, Leinster, and flows through the counties of Wicklow, Kildare and Dublin. Another important river is the Boyne, which rises in the Bog of Allen, County Kildare, and flows out into the sea at Drogheda, County Louth. The northern part of Leinster lies in the central plain of Ireland. There are areas of marshland in the northwest. The central plain continues south into the Bog of Allen. The Leinster Chain, a range which includes the Dublin, Wicklow and Blackstairs Mountains, runs down the east side of the region. Its highest point is Lugnaquillia (926 metres).

▼ **The Bog of Allen**
Bogs are dug for peat, which can be used as garden compost, or burnt as fuel.

Important towns

Dublin is the province's largest city. It is capital of the republic, and has an airport, port and university. Other important ports and industrial towns are Dunleary, Dundalk and Drogheda, in County Louth. The town of Wexford, in the southeastern corner of Leinster, is a seaport on the estuary of the river Slaney. Nearby Rosslare has an artificial harbour for large vessels and ferry services to Fishguard, in South Wales.

COUNTY FACTS

**COUNTY CARLOW
(CONTAE CEATHARACH)**
Area: 895 sq km
Population: 40,958
Administrative centre: Carlow Town
Other key places: Leighlinbridge, Tullow

**COUNTY DUBLIN
(CONTAE ATHA CLEATH)**
Area: 522 sq km
Population: 1,020,796
Administrative centres: Dublin, Dun Laoghaire
Other key places: Howth, Skerries

**COUNTY KILDARE
(CONTAE CHILL DARA)**
Area: 1,695 sq km
Population: 116,015
Administrative centre: Naas
Other key places: Kildare Town, Newbridge

**COUNTY KILKENNY
(CONTAE CHILL CHOINNIGH)**
Area: 2,060 sq km
Population: 73,094
Administrative centre: Kilkenny City
Other key places: Graiguenamanagh, Thomastown

COUNTY LAOIS (CONTAE LAOGHIS)
Area: 1,720 sq km
Population: 53,270
Administrative centre: Portlaoise
Other key places: Abbeyleix, Mountmellick, Portarlington

COUNTY LONGFORD
Area: 1,045 sq km
Population: 31,491
Administrative centre: Longford Town
Other key places: Lanesborough

▶ **Sky flier**
Sugar Loaf Mountain and Mount Leinster are popular with hang-gliders and paragliders.

▶ **Peregrine falcon**

COUNTY LOUTH
(CONTAE LUGHBHAIDH)
Area: 820 sq km
Population: 91,618
Administrative centre: Dundalk
Other key places: Ardee,
Drogheda

COUNTY MEATH
(CONTAE NA MIDHE)
Area: 2,340 sq km
Population: 103,762.
Administrative centre: Navan
Other key places: Duleek, Kells,
Newgrange, Tara, Trim

COUNTY OFFALY
(CONTAE UABH FAILGHE)
Area: 2,000 sq km
Population: 59,806
Administrative centre:
Tullamore
Other key places: Banagher,
Birr, Clonmacnoise

COUNTY WESTMEATH
Area: 1,760 sq km
Population: 63,306
Administrative centre:
Mullingar
Other key places: Athlone

COUNTY WEXFORD
(CONTAE LOCH GARMAN)
Area: 2,350 sq km
Population: 102,456
Administrative centre:
Wexford Town
Other key places: Enniscorthy,
New Ross, Rosslare

COUNTY WICKLOW
(CONTAE CILL MHANTÁIN)
Area: 2,025 sq km
Population: 94,482
Administrative centre:
Wicklow Town
Other key places: Arklow, Bray

ANCIENT BEACON
The black-and-white-striped lighthouse at
Hook Head, County Wexford, is thought
to be the world's oldest. It dates back to
at least the 5th century.

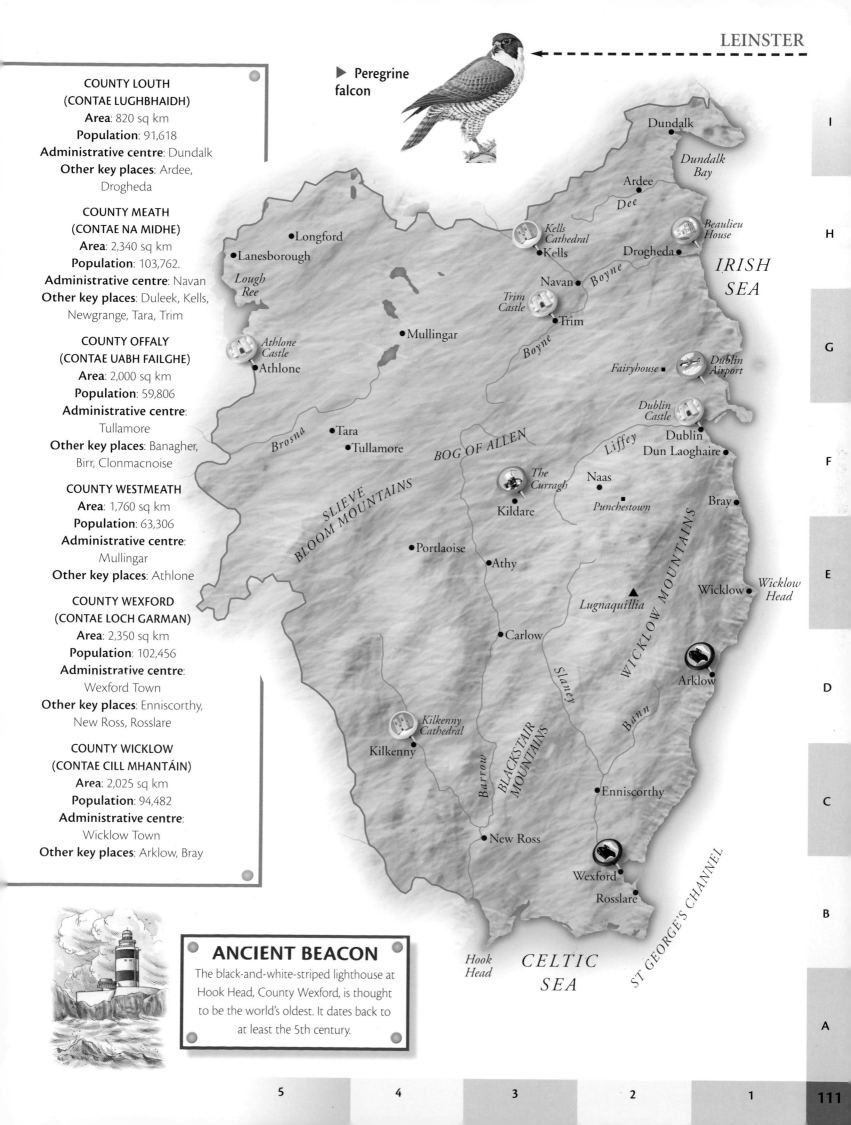

Map labels:

Dundalk
Dundalk Bay
Ardee
Dee
Beaulieu House
Longford
Kells Cathedral
Kells
Drogheda
IRISH SEA
Lanesborough
Navan
Boyne
Lough Ree
Trim Castle
Trim
Boyne
Mullingar
Dublin Airport
Athlone Castle
Athlone
Fairyhouse
Dublin Castle
Dublin
Brosna
Tara
BOG OF ALLEN
Liffey
Dun Laoghaire
Tullamore
Kildare
Naas
Bray
SLIEVE BLOOM MOUNTAINS
The Curragh
Punchestown
Portlaoise
Athy
Lugnaquillia
Wicklow
Wicklow Head
WICKLOW MOUNTAINS
Carlow
Slaney
Arklow
Kilkenny Cathedral
Kilkenny
Bann
Barrow
BLACKSTAIR MOUNTAINS
Enniscorthy
New Ross
Wexford
Hook Head
CELTIC SEA
ST GEORGE'S CHANNEL
Rosslare

ONE OF THE BURIAL MOUNDS at Tara is believed to be around 4,000 years old. Kilkenny has the remains of several Stone Age tombs, and an Iron Age fort.

▲ **Ancient remains**
There are stunning Stone Age remains in County Meath at Dowth, Knowth and Newgrange.

In the early history of Ireland, part of Leinster formed a fifth province, or kingdom, called Meath. Stretching from the river Shannon to the Irish Sea, it included present-day Meath and Westmeath, but it was swallowed up in the Middle Ages. The High Kings of Ireland once ruled from the sacred hill of Tara, in modern-day County Meath. The kings were crowned on the Stone of Destiny, which was later kept at Westminster Abbey and is now in Scotland.

THE EASTER RISING
The British Government had promised that Ireland would have home rule in 1914, but they postponed its introduction because of the start of World War I. Impatient at the delay, on April 24th, 1916 (Easter Monday), a group of republicans started a rebellion in Dublin. Led by Patrick Pearse and Tom Clarke, they seized the General Post Office and other buildings. The uprising was suppressed at the cost of more than 400 lives, including 230 civilians. Fifteen rebel leaders were executed.

◀ **The *Book of Kells***
The market town of Kells is an important religious site. There, monks produced the *Book of Kells*, one of the world's finest illuminated manuscripts. It is preserved at Trinity College, Dublin.

The English arrive

From 1042 the rulers of Leinster were members of the MacMurrough family. Dermot MacMurrough became king in 1126. His daughter, Eva, married a Norman baron, the Earl of Pembroke, nicknamed Strongbow. Dermot was banished from Ireland, and sought help from his son-in-law. Strongbow landed at Wexford, and with the aid of Norman allies conquered much of Ireland. This was the beginning of the English occupation of the island.

Castles

There are fine castles in Leinster, notably at Athlone, Ferns and Enniscorthy. Kilkenny City has a 12th-century castle and County Kildare boasts the ruins of more than 100 castles. Louth contains the ruins of several Norman castles. Many of the exploits of the mythical hero Cuchulain were supposed to have taken place in Louth.

◀ **Battling it out**
At the famous Battle of the Boyne in 1690, the Protestant William III finally defeated the Catholic James II, an event still celebrated by the Protestants of Northern Ireland.

WHAT'S IN A NAME?

Offaly was named King's County in 1556 after Philip II of Spain, the husband of Mary I of England. It resumed its ancient name in 1922. During the same period Laois was known as Queen's County, after Mary.

▼ World-famous stout

Guinness has been brewed in Dublin since 1759. This photo from the 1950s shows barrels of the stout being loaded on to barges on the Liffey.

Industry

Lanesborough, on Lough Ree, has a power station fuelled by peat. Laoise has a coalfield which produces anthracite. There is a large lead and zinc mine near Navan, and there are stone quarries across the province. Offaly has a variety of industries, mostly connected with agricultural produce. Arklow is an industrial town, with chemical plants.

Farming

Most of Leinster is devoted to agriculture. Farmers keep cattle, sheep and pigs. They grow cereal crops, potatoes, sugarbeet, fruit, vegetables and animal feed.

Fishing and horse-racing

The waters off the coast are rich fishing grounds. Catches include cod, herring and shellfish, such as lobsters and prawns. The National Stud of Ireland is at Tully, in County Kildare. Kildare is Ireland's flattest county – ideal for horse-racing. As well as the Curragh racecourse near Kildare Town, there are racecourses at Naas, Punchestown and Fairyhouse.

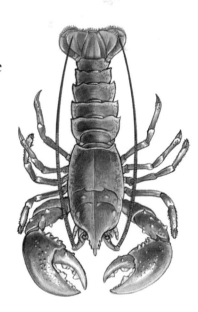

▲ Food from the sea

CAN YOU FIND?

1 Athlone Castle	4 Kells
2 Bog of Allen	5 Navan
3 The Curragh	6 Tara

see page 111

▼ A day at the races

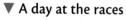

Munster

COUNTY FACTS

COUNTY CLARE (CONTAE CHLÁIR)
Area: 3,188 sq km
Population: 91,343
Administrative centre: Ennis
Other key places: Lisdoonvara, Shannon, Spanish Point

COUNTY CORK (CONTAE CHORCAIGHE)
Area: 7,422 sq km
Population: 279,427
Administrative centre: Cork City
Other key places: Bantry, Blarney, Clonakilty, Mallow

MUNSTER COVERS THE SOUTHWEST of the island and occupies one-third of the Irish Republic. The province has scenic landscapes, including the beautiful Lakes of Killarney, which are one of Ireland's biggest tourist attractions.

▼ **Wild landscape**
Killarney National Park, Kerry, covers 10,236 hectares.

Munster's coastline on the Atlantic Ocean is very rocky. Deep indents form numerous inlets and bays. County Limerick has a coastline on the Shannon Estuary. Around the town of Killarney in Kerry are the three Lakes of Killarney: Lough Leane, Muckross Lake and Upper Lake. Together with the surrounding woodland and Mountains of Kerry, they make up Killarney National Park. Munster consists mostly of moorland and highland, and includes the Republic's highest mountain, Carrauntoohil (1,040 metres), in the MacGillycuddy Reeks. From Limerick City, on the Shannon, running eastwards into County Waterford, is a region of rich, fertile farmland known as the Golden Vale. In the north of the province, County Clare forms a peninsula which is cut off from the rest of Munster by Lough Derg and the river Shannon.

▼ **Rare toad**
Natterjack toads can be found behind Inch Strand near Castle Gregory, County Kerry. The area is also home to the spotted Kerry slug.

▼ **Swiss Cottage**
This gorgeous thatched cottage, surrounded by flowers, is in Cahir Park, County Tipperary. Its architect was John Nash, who also designed Regent's Park, London.

Loop Head

Shan

Kerry Head

Important towns
Most of Munster is rural, but more people live in the towns than in rural areas. County Kerry, the westernmost county of Ireland, has one of the largest groups of Gaelic speakers although their number is declining. The province's main towns are Cork, Waterford and Limerick. Both Cork and Waterford have good natural harbours – Cork Harbour is one of the finest in Europe. The Cove of Cork in the harbour is a naval base, dockyard and seaport. Waterford City is Ireland's largest container port. Shannon is a new town that has developed around Shannon International Airport.

▼ **Rock of Cashel**
According to one legend, the huge Rock of Cashel in County Tipperary was bitten out of Devil's Bit Mountain by the devil himself. Cashel means 'fortress.'

▶ **Clare's coast**
In County Clare the Cliffs of Moher, which have a sheer, 180-metre drop, run for about eight kilometres along the coast.

Trale Bay

Gt Blasket Island

Dingle Bay

Valencia Island

MACGIL CUDI REE

Skellig Rocks

Kenmare River

CAHA MOUNT

Dunn

Mizen Hea

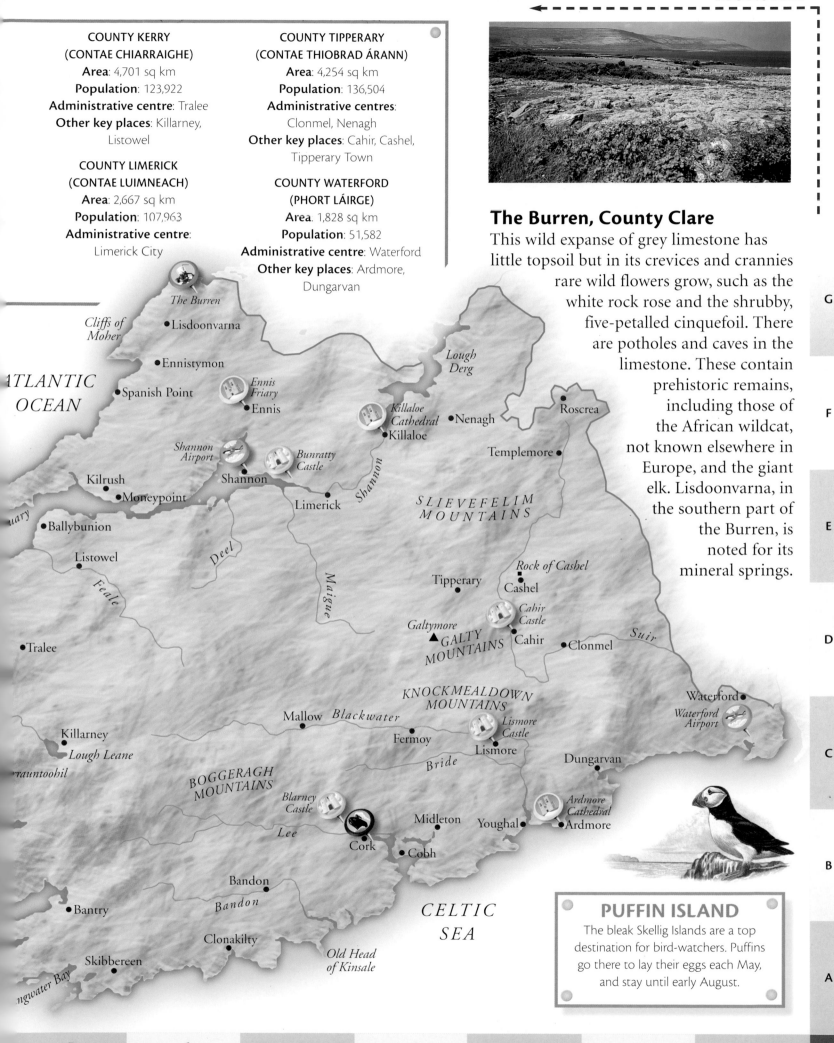

COUNTY KERRY
(CONTAE CHIARRAIGHE)
Area: 4,701 sq km
Population: 123,922
Administrative centre: Tralee
Other key places: Killarney,
Listowel

COUNTY LIMERICK
(CONTAE LUIMNEACH)
Area: 2,667 sq km
Population: 107,963
Administrative centre:
Limerick City

COUNTY TIPPERARY
(CONTAE THIOBRAD ÁRANN)
Area: 4,254 sq km
Population: 136,504
Administrative centres:
Clonmel, Nenagh
Other key places: Cahir, Cashel,
Tipperary Town

COUNTY WATERFORD
(PHORT LÁIRGE)
Area. 1,828 sq km
Population: 51,582
Administrative centre: Waterford
Other key places: Ardmore,
Dungarvan

The Burren, County Clare

This wild expanse of grey limestone has little topsoil but in its crevices and crannies rare wild flowers grow, such as the white rock rose and the shrubby, five-petalled cinquefoil. There are potholes and caves in the limestone. These contain prehistoric remains, including those of the African wildcat, not known elsewhere in Europe, and the giant elk. Lisdoonvarna, in the southern part of the Burren, is noted for its mineral springs.

PUFFIN ISLAND
The bleak Skellig Islands are a top destination for bird-watchers. Puffins go there to lay their eggs each May, and stay until early August.

Map labels:

The Burren
Cliffs of Moher
Lisdoonvarna
Ennistymon
ATLANTIC OCEAN
Spanish Point
Ennis Friary
Ennis
Lough Derg
Killaloe Cathedral
Killaloe
Nenagh
Roscrea
Shannon Airport
Bunratty Castle
Templemore
Kilrush
Moneypoint
Shannon
Limerick
SLIEVEFELIM MOUNTAINS
Ballybunion
Deel
Maigue
Shannon
Listowel
Feale
Rock of Cashel
Tipperary
Cashel
Galtymore
GALTY MOUNTAINS
Cahir Castle
Cahir
Clonmel
Suir
Tralee
KNOCKMEALDOWN MOUNTAINS
Waterford
Waterford Airport
Killarney
Lough Leane
rauntoohil
Mallow
Blackwater
Fermoy
Lismore Castle
Lismore
Dungarvan
Bride
BOGGERAGH MOUNTAINS
Blarney Castle
Midleton
Youghal
Ardmore Cathedral
Ardmore
Lee
Cork
Cobh
Bandon
Bandon
Bantry
CELTIC SEA
Clonakilty
Skibbereen
Old Head of Kinsale
ngwater Bay

G F E D C B A

THE LITTLE MARKET TOWN OF BRUFF, about 25 kilometres south of Limerick City, was the site of the earliest-known farms in Ireland. Stone Age remains from around 3000BC have been found. There are Bronze Age remains in County Clare.

The medieval history of Munster began in the 5th century AD, when the region was divided into a number of small Christian kingdoms. Cashel was a stronghold of the ancient kings of Munster who were crowned there. Waterford was invaded in the 900s by the Vikings, who founded Waterford City, and in the 1100s by the Normans. Despite these invasions, the Irish people of the region have retained their identity, and the western part of the county is a stronghold of Gaelic speakers.

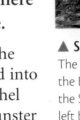

▲ Sacred stones
The first people settled in the Burren at the end of the Stone Age. They have left behind over 60 tombs.

THE BLARNEY STONE
According to legend, the triangular stone set into the wall of Blarney Castle, near Cork, has magical properties. Anyone who kisses it gains very strong powers of persuasion! The stone has been there since 1446.

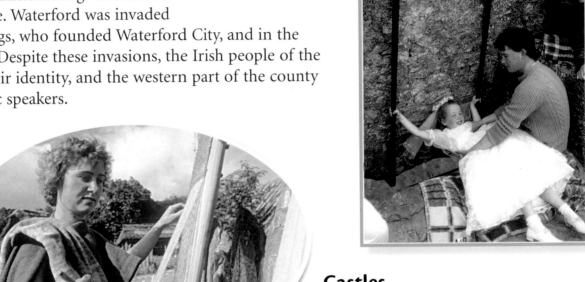

▶ Weaving history
At Bunratty Folk Park, County Clare, there is a reconstructed traditional Irish village. There are working weavers, blacksmiths and butter-makers.

Castles

Lough Gurr, near Limerick City, has two ruined castles on its banks. They were originally built on artificial islands called crannogs. Most of what survives of Bunratty Castle, on the road between Limerick and Ennis, was built in the 1400s. Clare has a number of medieval round towers. The monastic site of Ardmore, County Waterford, has a fine round stone tower. Towers like this were used as watchtowers and as hiding places for monastic treasures. There is a castle at Lismore, on the river Blackwater. Cahir Castle, with its huge keep and large courtyard, dominates the small town of Cahir in County Tipperary.

◀ At Spanish Point
Ships of the Spanish Armada were wrecked off the coast of County Clare. At Cnoc na Crocaire (hill of the gallows), 60 Armada survivors were hung.

◄ **Power provider**
Moneypoint power station
burns two million tonnes
of coal each year.
It supplies 40 percent of
the country's electricity.

▼ **Competitors,
Irish dancing**

MUSIC AND DANCE
Traditional Irish dancing was made
popular by the worldwide success of
the dance show, *Riverdance*. Irish jigs
are accompanied by folk music, usually
performed by a simple quartet
of musicians, who play the fiddle,
tin whistle, a goat-skin drum called
a *bodhrán*, and *uileann* pipes.

Industry
Industry has grown up around the Limerick
airport and the nearby city. There is a large
oil refinery in Cork Harbour, and an
offshore natural gasfield supplies people and
industry in and around the city. Ireland's
largest power station is coal-fired
Moneypoint near the village of Killimer,
County Clare. Other industries in County
Cork are based on agriculture. Hunting,
angling, climbing and tourism are
important to Munster's economy. Another
important industry is glass-making, centred
in Waterford City.

Farming and wildlife
There is good farmland in the river valleys of Munster
and on parts of the uplands, while large areas are
rough pasture. Agriculture is the main
activity, with the emphasis on rearing
cattle, pigs and sheep. Potatoes, oats,
wheat and sugarbeet are the main
crops, plus beets called mangel-
wurzels used for cattle feed.

▼ **Waterford**
Here, glass-blowers,
cutters and engravers
produce lead-crystal
glassware that is
world-famous.

▲ **Black pudding**
The town of Clonakilty, County Cork,
is famous for its delicious black pudding.
This sausage is made from pigs' blood.

◄ **Hung out to dry**
The village of Quilty,
County Clare, is a
centre for seaweed
production. Kelp and
other marine plants
are collected, dried
and processed for
use in toothpaste,
beer, agar and
cosmetics.

CAN YOU FIND?
1 Blarney Castle   4 Rock of Cashel
2 The Burren   5 Spanish Point
3 Clonakilty   6 Waterford

see pages 114 and 115

Ulster

▼ Donegal
Donegal, on the Atlantic coast, has fine, sandy beaches and beautiful scenery.

THE NORTHERN PART OF THE PROVINCE of Ulster has some of Ireland's most spectacular coastline. Ulster used to be made up of nine counties. The mainly Protestant 'six counties' of Ulster split off from the rest of Ireland in 1921 to form Northern Ireland. The three remaining (mostly Roman Catholic) Ulster counties formed part of the new, independent Republic of Ireland.

Donegal, whose Gaelic name means 'fort of the strangers', is cut off from the other two counties. Its coast is rocky, with many bays and inlets. The biggest is Donegal Bay in the south. Lough Foyle lies on Donegal's border with Londonderry. The most northerly point of Ireland is Malin Head, a name familiar to anyone who listens to the shipping forecast. The Derryveagh Mountains and the Blue Stack Mountains are both in County Donegal, too. Further south, Cavan and Monaghan form part of Ireland's central plain of farmland. Cavan is crossed with uplands and deep valleys. Monaghan is a region of rolling hills, small lakes and peat bogs. Slieve Beagh is a bleak, boggy range of hills, rising to 383 metres.

▲ Famine victims
This statue commemorates the people who starved to death in the terrible Potato Famine (1845–9). The famine was caused by a fungus that spoilt the potato crop for several years running. Over a million people died and about 1.5 million emigrated.

▲ Horse-riding in Donegal Bay

Industry, farming and fishing
Donegal is highly-industrialized. Almost half the people work in textile or clothing factories, and many of the rest in service industries. Cavan and Monaghan have few large towns, but these have food-processing and clothing factories. Ulster farmers rear cattle, pigs and poultry and grow oats, barley and potatoes. Fishing is a flourishing industry.

◄ Chicken
Poultry is raised to provide eggs and meat.

▲ Lace-making
A traditional craft in Donegal is sewing delicate lace by hand.

► Rock pools
The town of Bundoran is Donegal's most popular seaside resort.

◄ Beehive hut
This prehistoric stone hut is at Fahan, Donegal.

COUNTY FACTS

**COUNTY CAVAN
(CONTAE CABHÁN)**
Area : 1,891 sq km
Population: 53,881
Administrative centre:
Cavan Town

**COUNTY DONEGAL
(CONTAE DUN NA NGALL)**
Area: 4,830 sq km
Population: 129,428
Administrative centre:
Lifford
Other key places:
Bundoran, Donegal,
Killybegs

**COUNTY MONAGHAN
(CONTAE MUINEACHÁN)**
Area: 1,291 sq km
Population: 52,332
Administrative centre:
Monaghan Town
Other key places:
Castleblayney, Clones

▶ **Donegal tweed**
Tweed is a rough, woollen cloth woven on a loom. Donegal is famous for the fabric and has its own unique pattern.

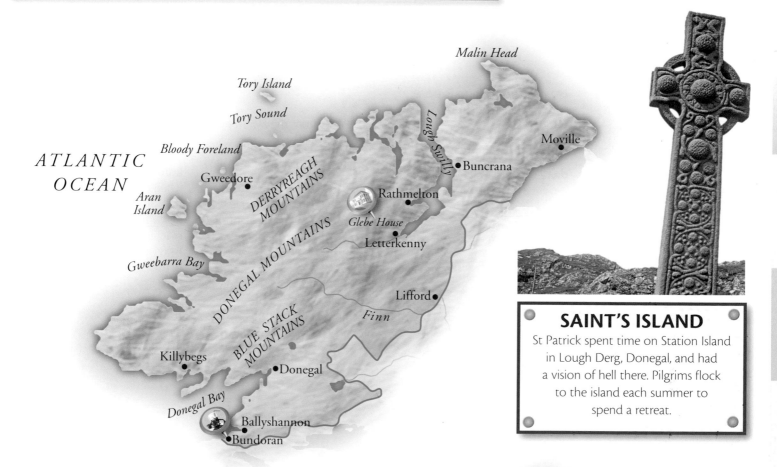

Malin Head

Tory Island

Tory Sound

*ATLANTIC
OCEAN*

Bloody Foreland

Gweedore

Aran
Island

DERRYREAGH
MOUNTAINS

Rathmelton

Lough Swilly

Moville

Buncrana

Glebe House

Letterkenny

DONEGAL MOUNTAINS

Gweebarra Bay

Lifford

Finn

BLUE STACK
MOUNTAINS

Killybegs

Donegal

Donegal Bay

Ballyshannon

Bundoran

SAINT'S ISLAND
St Patrick spent time on Station Island in Lough Derg, Donegal, and had a vision of hell there. Pilgrims flock to the island each summer to spend a retreat.

Moments in history
Donegal's remoteness saved it from serious invasion by the Normans, and during the 1500s and 1600s fewer Scots and English settled here than in the more eastern parts of Ulster. It remained a stronghold of spoken Gaelic when other parts of Ireland were speaking English. Monaghan escaped being part of the plantation of Ulster because the English government had already divided its land among eight Irish chiefs. The populations of both Cavan and Monaghan were seriously reduced by the Potato Famine of 1845–9.

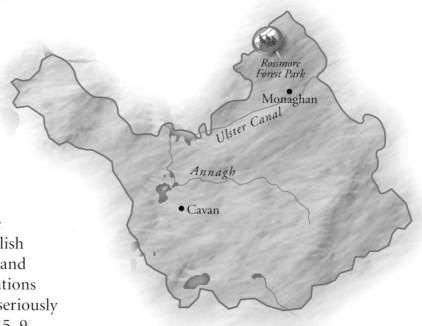

Rossmore
Forest Park

Monaghan

Ulster Canal

Annagh

Cavan

Glossary

Act of Union A law passed in parliament to join two (or more) countries together.

Anglo Saxon Relating to the Germanic peoples (including Angles, Saxons and Jutes) who settled England and Scotland.

anthracite Smokeless coal.

arable Describes land used for growing crops rather than, for example, raising cows or sheep.

basalt A type of very hard, dark-coloured igneous rock.

botanic garden A garden where (often rare) plants are cultivated, studied and displayed to the public; also called a botanical garden.

Bronze Age The prehistoric time after the Stone Age, lasting from around 2300BC until 700BC, when people used bronze for tools and weapons.

devolution A type of home rule, where some parts of government are controlled locally instead of by the national parliament.

canal A man-made river, usually almost perfectly flat, that can be used to transport goods by boat.

causeway A raised road or pathway, for example over marshy land, or across a stretch of sea.

Celt A member of one of the prehistoric tribes of farmers that settled Britain and Ireland during the Iron Age. Celtic languages, such as Gaelic, are still alive today in Ireland, Wales, the Scottish Highlands and the Isle of Man.

clan Like a tribe, a group of people led by a single chieftain, especially in the Scottish Highlands. Clan members are often related and share the same surname.

climate The average weather of a place throughout the year.

coalfield An area that has strata, or layers, of coal. Coal is a rock that formed millions of years ago from long-decayed vegetation.

continental drift The gradual movement of the Earth's land masses that breaks up existing continents and forms new ones.

crannog Gaelic word describing an artifical island on which a dwelling or fort has been built.

croft A smallholding, usually consisting of a tiny farm with a cottage; its owner is called a crofter.

cromlech A prehistoric stone structure, such as a tomb or standing stones.

currency A country's money.

dairy cattle Cows raised to produce milk, rather than beef.

dale Low-lying ground between hills; often, this is a river valley.

dam A large wall or bank built to hold back river water and raise its level.

depression A moving area of low air pressure where storms are common.

Depression Period during the 1930s when the economy was poor and there was a great deal of unemployment and hardship.

distilling Process of purifying an alcoholic drink, such as whisky, by evaporating and condensing it.

dolmen A prehistoric stone structure, probably used as a tomb. It usually consisted of several standing stones with a flat stone placed on top.

downs Gently-sloping, treeless hillsides, or uplands.

earthwork A mound of earth used in prehistoric times as a fort.

embankment A bank or mound of earth.

erode To wear away the land. Wind, moving water and glaciers all erode the land.

escarpment The steep side of a hill, cliff or rock.

estuary The part of a river where it reaches the sea and often has tides; the river's mouth.

fault A crack in the rocks that form the Earth's crust. Fault lines are likely spots for earthquakes or volcanoes.

fell A hill, usually of uncultivated land such as pasture or moor.

fenland Low-lying marshy land, often covered with water.

firth The mouth of a river or an arm of the sea.

fishery A place where fish are caught.

flax Fibres from the *Linum* plant, used to make linen.

ford Part of a river that is shallow enough to wade across.

game Wild animals killed for food or sport, such as deer (for venison meat), geese or rabbits.

gasfield An area that has deposits of natural gas.

gavelkind A system of inheritence whereby a dead man's property is divided equally between all his son or, if he has no sons, his daughters.

glacier A large sheet of ice, or ice and rock, that flows slowly down a valley like a frozen river.

glen A narrow, often wooded, valley.

gorge A deep, narrow canyon that cuts through the land.

government The institution that controls the country. It sets laws and enforces them and manages relations with other countries.

granite A type of very hard, speckled igneous rock.

grove A small area of woodland.

Gulf Stream Warm water current that originates in the Gulf of Mexico and flows across the Atlantic to northwestern Europe.

headland A point of land that juts out into the sea.

hill fort A prehistoric stronghold on top of a hill.

home rule Self-government, as opposed to rule by another country.

hot spring A spring of water that has been heated underground by volcanic activity.

hummock A small hill.

hydroelectric power Energy made by harnessing the movement of water, either downhill or in tides or waves.

igneous Describes a rock formed when volcanic lava cooled. Granite and basalt are both igneous rocks.

Industrial Revolution Period when the first factories were built. Instead of human labour, newly-invented, steam-powered machines performed repetitive or heavy tasks. In Britain, this began in the 1760s.

inlet A small bay in a coastline.

Iron Age The prehistoric time after the Bronze Age, beginning around 700BC, when people used iron tools and weapons.

islet A tiny island.

kirk A Scottish word for 'church.'

limestone A type of easily-eroded rock, such as chalk, that formed millions of years ago from the crushed shells and skeletons of tiny sea creatures.

loch Pronounced 'lock'. This is a Gaelic word meaning 'lake.' A loch may contain fresh or salt water.

lough Pronounced 'lock'. The Irish version of 'loch,' that is, a lake.

Loyalist A person who is loyal to the monarch. In Northern Ireland, Loyalists are people who would like the province to remain part of the United Kingdom.

managed forest Trees planted rather like a crop to be harvested for their timber. Felled trees are replaced with new saplings.

marina A harbour or dock where yachts are berthed.

market garden A garden where fruit, vegetables and flowers are grown for sale to the public.

medieval From the Middle Ages.

Middle Ages The time between the end of the Roman empire in the AD400s, until the explosion of invention and learning in the 1400s, known as the Renaissance.

mint A place where money is printed or coined.

monarch A head of state, for example a king or queen, who inherits their title.

moorland An expanse of wild, uncultivated land, which often has poor, peaty soil.

motte-and-bailey castle A type of castle built by the Normans, where the tower, or keep, is built on an earth mound (motte), surrounded by a walled courtyard (bailey).

mya Million years ago

national assembly An assembly of elected representatives that governs a country, or aspects of a country.

nuclear power Energy produced when atoms such as uranium or plutonium are split in carefully-controlled conditions.

oil platform A steel or concrete structure supporting an oil rig out at sea. Some platforms are free-floating; others are fixed to the seabed.

oil rig The machinery and structures used to drill for oil.

outcrop Rock that is visible at the surface, rather than hidden under the soil.

paramilitary Describes a rebel group that is organized like an army.

parliament The seat of government. Some members of parliament are elected by the people (in Britain, they attend the House of Commons; in the Republic of Ireland, they attend the Dáil); others are born or appointed to a position in the upper house (in Britain, this is the House of Lords; in the Republic of Ireland, this is the Senate).

patron saint A saint considered to be protector of a country.

peat bog Marshy land where peat has formed. Peat is long-decayed vegetation, the first step in the process that produces coal.

pele tower A simple, fortified house, often entered by means of a ladder to the first floor.

peninsula A large strip of land that juts into the sea.

Pict A prehistoric Celtic people that inhabited northeastern Scotland.

plain An area of flat or gently-undulating land, that is usually low-lying.

plantation of Ireland The settling of Ireland from the 1600s by English and Scottish people, so Britain could establish control.

plate A large section of the Earth's crust. Plates are constantly moving against each other.

plateau A area of level, high ground.

plug Rock that has hardened inside a volcano's central hole, or vent.

pothole A deep hole eroded in limestone.

prehistoric From the time before there were any written historical records.

prevailing wind The wind that blows most often in a particular place or region.

principality A territory ruled by a prince or princes.

Protestant Church A branch of Christianity that has separated from the Roman Catholic Church. Protestant churches first formed during the Reformation.

province A distinct part of a country, treated differently to the rest of the country.

quarry A site where rock is dug or blown out of the ground. Quarried rocks are mostly used for building and include sandstone and slate.

rain shadow An area that is sheltered from prevailing winds by hills or mountains. As a result, it has lower rainfall than the windward side of the mountains.

rayon Man-made silk, manufactured from cellulose, which is a chemical found in plant pulp.

reef A chain of underwater rocks, usually closer to the surface than the surrounding seabed.

refinery A place where raw ingredients are processed, for example an oil or sugar refinery.

Reformation Period in the 1500s when the Church underwent changes. Before then, the only Christian Church was the Roman Catholic one; during the 1500s, various Protestant churches sprang up.

regeneration The creation of new buildings and businesses in a place.

republic A country without a monarch as head of state, that is governed entirely by elected representatives of the people.

Republican A person who believes that a republic is the best form of government. In Northern Ireland, Republicans are people who would like the province to become part of the Republic of Ireland.

reserve An area of land put aside for a special use, such as conserving wildlife.

reservoir A man-made lake.

Roman Catholic Church The first Christian Church, headed by the Pope in Rome. Catholic means 'universal.'

rune A symbol that is a character, or letter, from one of the alphabets used by Germanic peoples between the 3rd and 13th centuries.

slate Shiny, green- or blue-grey rock made up of thin plates, often used for roofing tiles.

smallholding A small plot of land, usually used for farming.

smelting Melting ore to separate out the metal, such as aluminium.

smokehouse A place where meat, fish or cheese is smoked, usually over a wood fire.

solar power Energy from the Sun.

solstice The day that the Sun is farthest away from the Equator. This happens twice in a year on the longest and shortest days, June 21st and December 21st.

stack An isolated pillar of rock, usually poking out of the sea.

standing stone A huge stone set upright in the ground. They were erected by prehistoric peoples, probably for religious purposes.

steelworks A factory where iron is transformed into steel.

Stone Age The prehistoric time before the Bronze Age, from around 4000BC until 2300BC, when people used tools and weapons made of stone, such as flint. The period is split into the Old Stone Age (Paleolithic) and New Stone Age (Neolithic).

stone circle A ring of prehistoric standing stones.

supertanker A huge boat that carries a liquid cargo, such as oil.

suspension bridge A bridge with its deck supported from above by large cables or chains hanging from towers.

taoiseach Pronounced 'tee-shock.' The prime minister of the Republic of Ireland.

terrorism Organized violence, usually with the purpose of bringing about political change.

tributary A stream or river that flows into – and becomes part of – another, larger river.

tweed Rough, woollen cloth. Much of it is produced in the valley of the river Tweed.

viaduct A road or rail bridge over a valley.

Viking A Scandinavian people who invaded or raided parts of Britain between the AD700s and 1000s.

volcano A vent in the Earth's crust, out of which molten rock, ashes and steam erupt.

wetland Marshy land.

wold A low hill.

Gazetteer

MAP CO-ORDINATES

Co-ordinates provide a way to find a place on a map. On each map page there is a border at the bottom that is divided into numbered blocks, and a border at the edge that is divided into lettered blocks. Together with the page number, these border numbers and letters are used to create the co-ordinates.

How do I give a place on a map its own co-ordinates?

1 Write down the page that the place is on. This is the first co-ordinate. If you want co-ordinates for Glasgow, then '79' is the first part, because Glasgow appears on the map on page 79.

2 Next put your finger on the place itself. Trace down to the bottom of the page and see which numbered block you reach. This number is the second co-ordinate. In the case of Glasgow, you reach number '4.'

3 Now put your finger back on the place and trace across to the edge of the page to see which lettered block you reach. This is the last co-ordinate. In the case of Glasgow, you reach letter 'D.'

4 Write down the three co-ordinates, separating them with commas so that they don't get muddled together. The co-ordinates for Glasgow would be '79, 4, D.'

How do I use co-ordinates to find a place on a map?

1 All the places listed alphabetically in the Gazetteer have three co-ordinates. Look up the place name and read its co-ordinates. If you look up Glasgow, you read '79, 4, D.'

2 The first co-ordinate refers to the page that the place is on, so turn to that page. To find Glasgow, you would turn to page 79.

3 It's easiest to work with the second and third co-ordinates at the same time. The second co-ordinate refers to a number on the border at the bottom of the page. Place a finger on the block of border with that number in it. The third co-ordinate refers to a letter at the edge of the page. Place a finger in the block of border with that letter in it. In the case of Glasgow, you would have one finger on the number '4' and one on the letter 'D.'

4 Now move the finger on the number upwards and the finger on the letter to the left. The imaginary square where they meet will contain the place you were looking for.

See County Facts boxes on map pages

Place	Co-ordinates
Aberdeen, Aber	87, 4, E
Aberystwyth, Cerdgn	57, 3, F
Antrim, Antrm	103, 3, D
Armagh, Armgh	103, 4, B
Aylesbury, Bucks	23, 7, C
Ayr, S Ayrs	79, 4, C
Bedford, Beds	31, 3, B
Belfast, Belf	103, 2, C
Berwick-upon-Tweed, Nthumb	47, 4, H
Birmingham, W Mids	27, 4, D
Blackpool, Lancs	39, 4, G
Bradford, W York	43, 6, C
Brighton, E Susx	19, 5, B
Bristol, Gloucs	15, 3, F
Caernarfon, Gwynd	53, 5, D
Caerphilly, Caerph	61, 5, B
Cambridge, Cambs	31, 2, B
Canterbury, Kent	19, 2, D
Cardiff, Cardif	61, 5, A
Carlisle, Cumb	47, 6, E
Carlow, Carl	111, 3, D
Carmarthen, Carmth	61, 8, C
Carrick-on-Shannon, Leit	109, 2, E
Castlebar, Mayo	109, 5, E
Cavan, Cav	119, 3, B
Chelmsford, Essex	23, 4, C
Chester, Ches	39, 3, E
Chichester, W Susx	19, 7, B
Conwy, Conwy	53, 4, E
Cork, Cork	115, 4, B
Coventry, W Mids	27, 3, D
Cwmbran, Mons	61, 4, B
Doncaster, S York	43, 4, B
Dorchester, Dorset	15, 3, D
Douglas, IoM	65, 2, B
Dover, Kent	19, 1, C
Downpatrick, Down	103, 2, B
Dublin, Dub	111, 1, F
Dumbarton, W Duns	79, 4, E
Dumfries, D&G	73, 3, E
Dunbar, E Loth	77, 1, F
Dundalk, Louth	111, 2, I
Dundee, Dund	85, 3, D
Durham, Dur	47, 3, E
Edinburgh, Edin	77, 3, F
Elgin, Moray	87, 6, G
Ennis, Clare	115, 5, F
Enniskillen, Ferm	103, 6, B
Exeter, Devon	15, 6, D
Falkirk, Falk	83, 5, D
Felixstowe, Suffk	35, 4, C
Fishguard, Pembks	61, 9, C
Forfar, Angus	85, 3, D
Fraserburgh, Aber	87, 4, G

Place	Co-ordinates
Galway, Glwy	109, 4, B
Gateshead, T&W	47, 3, E
Glasgow, Glas	79, 4, D
Glenrothes, Fife	85, 4, C
Gloucester, Gloucs	15, 2, H
Greenock, Inver	79, 5, E
Guildford, Surrey	19, 6, D
Hamilton, S Lans	79, 4, C
Harwich, Essex	23, 2, C
Hastings, E Susx	19, 3, B
Haverfordwest, Pembks	61, 9, C
Hereford, Herefd & Worcs	27, 6, C
Hertford, Herts	23, 5, C
Hull *see* Kingston-upon-Hull	
Inverness, Highld	89, 3, E
Ipswich, Suffk	35, 4, C
Irvine, N Ayrs	79, 5, C
Kilkenny, Kilk	111, 4, C
Kilmarnock, E Ayrs	79, 4, C
Kingston-upon-Hull, ER Yk	43, 2, C
Kirkintilloch, E Duns	79, 4, E
Kirkwall, Ork	93, 4, D
Lancaster, Lancs	39, 3, H
Leeds, W York	43, 5, C
Leicester, Leics	27, 2, E
Lerwick, Shet	95, 5, F
Lewes, E Susx	19, 5, B
Lifford, Don	119, 5, E
Limerick, Limrk	115, 5, E
Lincoln, Lincs	31, 3, F
Liverpool, Mersyd	39, 3, F
Llandrindod Wells, Powys	57, 2, E
Llangefni, IoA	53, 6, E
Lochgilphead, Ag & B	79, 6, E
London, Gt Lon	12
Londonderry, Lndrry	103, 5, E
Longford, Long	111, 5, H
Luton, Beds	31, 3, A
Maidstone, Kent	19, 3, D
Manchester, Gt Man	39, 2, F
Matlock, Derbys	27, 3, G
Melrose, Border	75, 5, D
Merthyr Tydfil, Myr Td	61, 5, B
Milford Haven, Pembks	61, 9, B
Milton Keynes, Bucks	23, 7, D
Mold, Flints	53, 3, D
Monaghan, Mon	119, 2, C
Morpeth, Nthumb	47, 3, F
Motherwell, N Lans	79, 3, D
Mullingar, Wmth	111, 4, G
Naas, Kild	111, 2, F
Navan, Meath	111, 3, H
Newbury, Berks	22, 8, A
Newcastle-upon-Tyne, T&W	47, 3, E

'CAN YOU FIND?' answers

England: the Southwest p17
1	Bristol	15, 3, F
2	Longleat House	15, 2, F
3	Lyme Regis	15, 4, D
4	St Ives	14, 11, B

England: the Southeast p21
1	Canterbury Cathedral	19, 2, D
2	Cowes	18, 8, B
3	Leeds Castle	19, 3, D
4	New Forest	18, 9, B
5	Thorpe Park	19, 6, D

England: South Central p24
1	Banbury	22, 8, D
2	Colchester	23, 3, C
3	Milton Keynes	23, 7, D
4	St Albans	23, 6, C
5	Windsor	23, 6, A

England: West Midlands p28
1	Eyam	27, 3, G
2	Loughborough	27, 2, E
3	Rugby	27, 2, D
4	Stratford-upon-Avon	27, 4, C
5	Worcester	27, 5, C

England: East Midlands p33
1	Ely Cathedral	31, 1, C
2	Sherwood Forest	31, 5, F
3	Silverstone	31, 4, B
4	Tattershall Castle	31, 3, F
5	Wisbech	31, 2, D

England: East Anglia p37
1	Bury St Edmunds	35, 6, D
2	Great Yarmouth	35, 3, E
3	Lavenham	35, 5, C
4	Sandringham House	35, 6, F
5	Little Walsingham	35, 5, F

England: the Northwest p40
1	Blackpool	39, 4, H
2	Chester	39, 3, E
3	Forest of Bowland	39, 3, H
4	Little Moreton Hall	39, 2, E
5	Manchester	39, 2, F
6	Morecambe	39, 3, H

England: the Northeast p45
1	Castle Howard	43, 4, D
2	Conisbrough Castle	43, 4, B
3	Halifax	43, 6, C
4	Sheffield	43, 5, A
5	York Minster	43, 4, C

England: the North p49
1	Durham Cathedral	47, 3, E
2	Kielder Water	47, 5, F
3	Newcastle-upon-Tyne	47, 3, E
4	Sellafield	47, 7, C
5	Windermere	47, 6, C

North Wales p54
1	Conwy Castle	53, 4, E
2	Holyhead	53, 6, E
3	Lake Bala	53, 4, C
4	Portmeirion	53, 5, C
5	Snowdon	53, 5, D

Mid Wales p59
1	Aberystwyth	57, 3, F
2	Brecon Beacons	57, 2, D
3	Hay-on-Wye	57, 1, D
4	Llanwrtyd Wells	57, 2, E
5	Powis Castle	57, 1, G

South Wales p62
1	Caerphilly Castle	61, 2, B
2	Cardiff	61, 2, A
3	Gower Peninsula	61, 4, B
4	Milford Haven	61, 6, B
5	Swansea Cathedral	61, 4, B

Scotland: Strathclyde p79
1	Dunstaffnage Castle	79, 6, G
2	Glasgow Cathedral	79, 4, D
3	Iona	78, 8, F
4	Loch Lomond	79, 4, E
5	Paisley	79, 4, D
6	Staffa	78, 8, F

Ireland: Northern Ireland p105
1	Armagh	103, 4, B
2	Belfast	103, 2, C
3	Bushmills	103, 3, E
4	Downpatrick Cathedral	103, 2, B
5	Slieve Donard	103, 2, A

Ireland: Leinster p113
1	Athlone Castle	111, 5, G
2	Bog of Allen	111, 4, F
3	The Curragh	111, 3, F
4	Kells	111, 3, H
5	Navan	111, 3, H
6	Tara	111, 5, F

Ireland: Munster p117
1	Blarney Castle	115, 5, B
2	The Burren	115, 6, G
3	Clonakilty	115, 6, A
4	Rock of Cashel	115, 3, E
5	Spanish Point	115, 7, F
6	Waterford	115, 1, C

ACKNOWLEDGEMENTS

The publishers would like to thank the following artists whose work appears in this title:

Lisa Alderton/Advocate, Vanessa Card, Kuo Kang Chen; Wayne Ford, Terry Gabbey/AFA Ltd., Jeremy Gower, Ron Hayward, Gary Hincks, Sally Holmes, Richard Hook/Linden Artists, The Maltings, Janos Marffy, Terry Riley, Andrew Robinson, Peter Sarson, Mike Saunders, Christian Webb/Temple Rogers, Mike White/Temple Rogers, John Woodcock

PHOTOGRAPHIC CREDITS

The publishers thank the following sources for the use of their photographs:

Page 8 (B/L) National Gallery, London, UK/ Bridgeman Art Library; 9 (L) Aled Hughes/The Photo Library Wales; 13 (T/L) Skyscan Photo Library; (B/L) Clare Oliver;(B/R) The Photo Library Wales;14 (C/L) London Aerial Photography/Corbis; 17 (C/L) Wookey Hole Caves Ltd.,(B/R) Aardman Animations Ltd; (T/R) David Alan-Williams; (C) Cordaiy Photo Library/Corbis; 18 (T/L) Colorsport; (C/L) South East England Tourist Board; 20 (C/L) Dover Harbour Board; 22 (T/L) Jean Hall/Sylvia Cordaiy Photo Library; (C/R) The Open University; 23 (T/L) IN-Press Photography; 24(T/L) Skyscan Photography; (B/L) Frank Spooner Pictures; 25 (T/L) Christine & John Burke; (B/L) Legoland, Windsor Park Ltd.; 26 (B/L) London Aerial Photo Library; 27 (B/C) Alton Towers;28 (T/L) David Toase/Travel Ink; 29 (B/R) Cadbury World; (T/C) Bridgeman Art Library; (C/R) Castrol, (C) Trustees of The Wedgwood Museum; 32 (T/L) The Ermine Street Guard; 33 (T/L) Chris Parker/Sylvia Cordaiy Photo Library; (B/L) Sutton Motorsport Images; (C/R) Airware UK Ltd.; 34 (T/L) Chris Parker/Sylvia Cordaiy Photo Library; (B) Paul Shawcross /Leslie Garland Picture Library; 35 (B/R) University of East Anglia; 36 (C/L) Roman Catholic National Shrine of Our Lady of Walsingham; 37 (B/L) Greene King; 38 (B/L) Colorsport 39 (C) Chester Zoo; (B/L) Colorsport; 40 (C/R) Colin Raw/Leslie Garland Picture Library; 41 (T/R) Corbis; (B/L) Abbie Enock/Travel Ink; (B/R) Colorsport (C/R) Abbie Enock/Travel Ink/Corbis; 42 (B/L) Colorsport; (B/R) Eureka!Museum; 43 (T/C) York Minster Library & Archives; 44 (T/R) G. Taunton/Sylvia Cordaiy Photo Library; (C/L) & (B/L) Castle Howard Estate Ltd.; 45 (B/L) David Mellor; (T/L) Hulton-Deutsch/Corbis; 46 (B/R) & (C/R) Leslie Garland; 47 (T/R) Chillingham Wild Cattle Association; 49 (T/L) Hulton-Deutsch/Corbis; (C) Forest Life Picture Library; (C/R) Trustees of The Wedgwood Museum (B/.L) B.N.F.L., Sellafield; 50 (T/R) Bibliotheque Nationale,Paris,France/ Bridgeman Art Library,51 (T/R) The Photo Library Wales; (B/L)Dave Williams/The Photo Library Wales,(T/L) Skyscan Photo Library; 53 (B/R) Portmeirion Village & Gardens; 55 (T/C) K.Morris/The Photo Library Wales, (C) Express Newspapers, (B/L) Steve Benbow/The Photo Library Wales; 56 (B) A.Hughes/The Photo Library Wales; 57 (T/L) A.Hughes/The Photo Library Wales, (B/L) The Photo Library Wales; 59 (T/L) The Neuadd Arms Hotel, (T/R) Centre for Alternative Technology, (B/R) & (B/L) Steve Benbow/The Photo Library Wales; 60 (B/R) The Photo Library Wales; 62 (T/L) CADW Photographic Library, 63 (T/L) Penguin UK; 65 (C/R) Island Photographics;66 (B/L) SantíEmidio, Ascoli Picena, Bridgeman Art Library; 67 (B/L)S.J.Taylor/Still Moving Picture Co.; 68 (T/R) Cairngorm Marketing; 70, (B/L) Doug Corrance/Still Moving Picture Co, (C/R) Ken Paterson/Still Moving Picture Co, (B/R) S.J.Taylor/Still Moving Picture Co;71 (C) S.J.Taylor/Still Moving Picture Co, (T/L)Skyscan;73 (B/L)Libby Withnall; (B/R) Macduff Everton/Corbis; 78 (B/R)Ian Britton, 80 (C/L) Glasgow Museums; 81 (B/L) Glasgow School of Art, (T/C); 83 (T/R) Falkirk Museum, (C/R) The National Wallace Monument; 85 (B/L) Angus Tourist Board, (B/R) D.C.Thomson & Co.Ltd; 87 (B/L) Glenfiddich Distillery; 88 (C/L) Caithness Glass Ltd., (C/R) West Highland Museum; 91 (B/L) Harris Tweed Assoc.; 92 all by Richard Welsby; 94 (C/R) British Petroleum Co., (B/L) Just Shetland, (T/L) Richard Welsby; 95 (B) Shetland Times;(C/R) Kevin Schafer/Corbis; 96 (T/L) Huntingdon Library & Art Gallery, San Marino, CA, USA/Bridgeman Art Library; (B/L)) Bettmann/Corbis, 97 (T/L) Hulton Deutsch/Corbis,(C) S.Rafferty/Eye Ubiquitous/Corbis,(B/L) Private collection/Bridgeman Art Library: 99 (B/R) Tom Bean/Corbis;100 (B/L) Michael St.Maur Sheil/Corbis, (T/R & T/C) from BSK Photo Library, (C/L) Sean Sexton Collection/Corbis; 101 (T/L) BSK Photo Library; 102 (C/R) & (B/L) A.Davis/Leslie Garland Picture Library, (B/R) J.Harpur/The National Trust Photographic Library; 104 (B/R) North Down Heritage Centre; (B/L) AFP/Corbis; 105 (T/L) Reproduced by kind permission of the Trustees of the National Museums & Galleries of Northern Ireland, (B/C) Bushmills; 106 (T/R) & (B/R) BSK Photo Library; 107 (C/R) BSK Photo Library,(T/R) Skyscan Photo Library; 107 (B/L) Iarnrod Eireann 108 (B/R) Abbie Enock/Travel Ink; 109 ((T/R) K.Dwyer/Skyscan Photo Library; 110 (C/L) A.Davies/Leslie Garland Picture Library; 112 (C/R)Hulton-Deutsch/Corbis; 113 (B) Creative Imprints, 113 (T/R) Guinness Ltd. 114 (T/L) K.Dwyer/Skyscan, (C/R) Jill Swainson/Travel Ink; 115 (T/L) Ken Gibson/Travel Ink; 116 (T/L) K.Dwyer/Skyscan Photo Library; 117 (T/L) Moneypoint Power Plant, (C) Brian Lynch/Bord Failte, (B/R) K.Dwyer/Skyscan Photo Library, (C/R) Irish Dancing Magazine; 118 (T/R), (C/L) Brian Lynch/Bord Failte, (B/R) Erne Enterprise Development Co. Ltd./Bundoran UDC; 119 (T/R) Abbie Enock/Travel Ink.

Every effort has been made to trace and credit all images used and the publishers apologise if any have been omitted.
All other photographs from MKP Archives